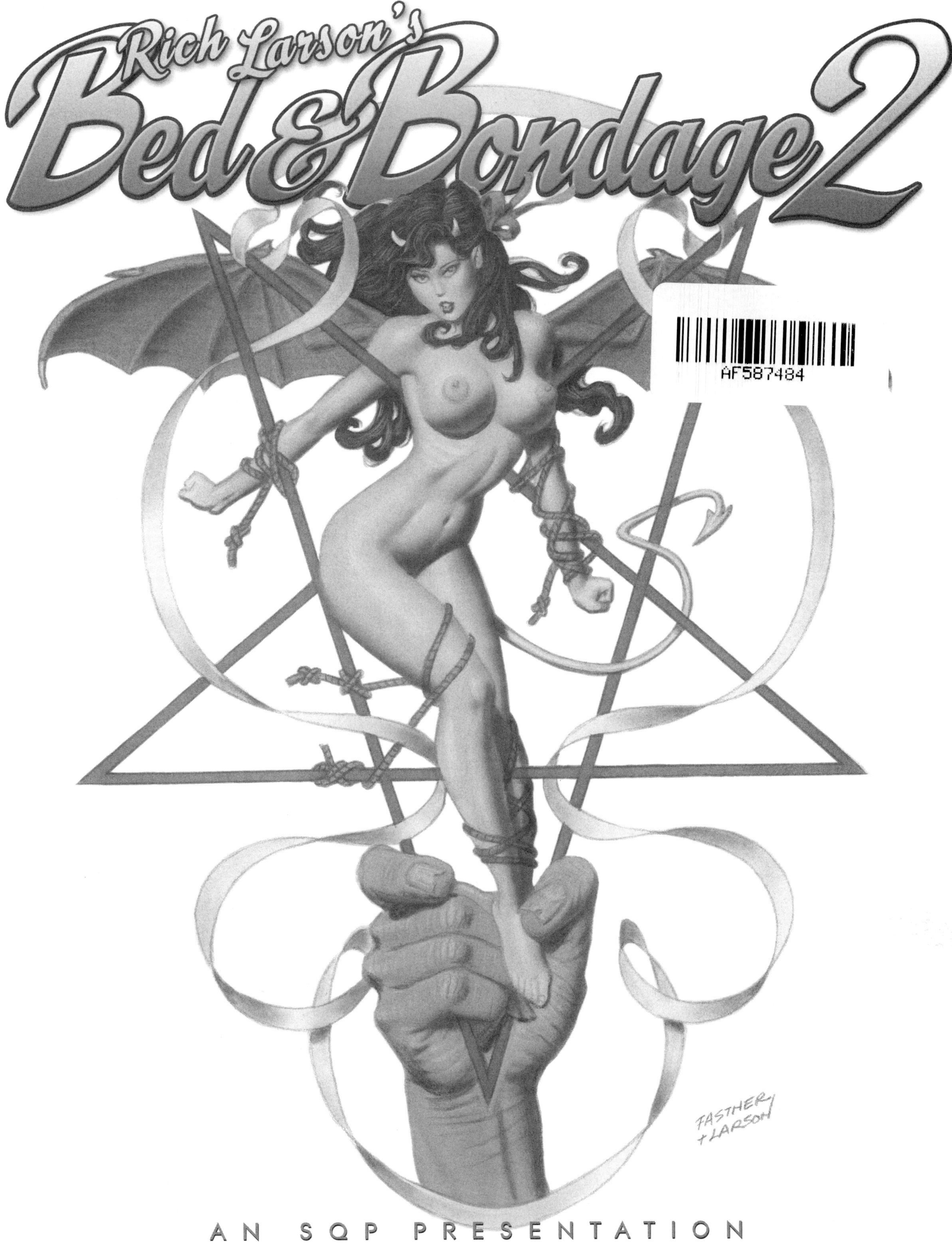
Rich Larson's
Bed & Bondage 2
FASTNER + LARSON
AN SQP PRESENTATION

Chained to the Fetish Boiler in Fantasy's Sub-Basement, Part Two

"Nicki dear can you hear me?" Vicki asked.

The trunk bowed slightly.

"I have to ask her," Vicki explained in an aside to me, "Sometimes she wears a discipline helmet with heavy padding over the ears and she can't quite hear a sound."

"...You know I went to the theatre?"

"Yes", bowed the trunk.

"I sat next to a very nice young man. I made an excuse to borrow his pencil and drop it. He looked like he might be interested in girls like us, so when he dived for the pencil, I pulled up my skirt and showed him my boots. As a result, he not only came back to the house to meet you, but he's got me tied to this chair and he's looking at you as though he'd like to eat you. If you want to say, 'Hello', he's just to the right of me here."

The trunk turned in my direction and the legs did a very nice curtsey

.

—**Bound in Leather 1**, 1953

Every century has its Mr. Bondage Art Guy, and it can reasonably be argued that the Twentieth's was Eric Stanton. From the mid forties through at least the nineties, Stanton has been an inexhaustible fount of fetish illustration — one with whom comics fans ought to have at least a passing acquaintance, since he studied cartooning under Jerry Robinson, and shared an art studio (and drawing style) with Steve Ditko.

Taschen's hernia-inducing Stanton retrospective is 352 uninterrupted 10 1/2" X 13 3/4" pages of dominant women, submissive men, submissive women, rubber masks, seven inch spike heels, maid outfits, ropes, chains, living suitcases, circus animals, catapults, leather corsets, straps, gears, and human golf tees.

Some of the imagery is a bit disquieting.

Nicki offered her smiling mask for a kiss, but before I took her up, I produced the thing I had had the jeweler make, it was a diamond engagement ring with a spring clasp fitted in the band. I clipped it on the septum of Nicki's nose.

"You can't wear it on your finger, for your arms will be behind you almost all the time, so I think a diamond nose-ring is a neat substitute, don't you?"

She nodded and offered her mask again. This time I obliged, and Nicki and I were engaged.

By comparison, **Bed & Bondage 2** (and **B&B 1**, for that matter — still available on six of the seven continents!) is pretty much brunch with the Daughters of the American Revolution.

In the present volume, we tip our hat to Stanton (or rip him off, depending on your point of view) in "Busman's Holiday", and he even makes a brief cameo appearance in "The Fun Couple".

(In **B&B 1**, the ingenious rat/spider torture idea of "Cheesed" is Stanton's. Now you have to get a copy of that to see what the hell we're talking about.)

But there's nothing in these pages even roughly analogous to his immortal **Hampered by Heather**, **Nurse in Rubber**, or **The Punished Publisher** — which we think may be about Bob and Sal. Those are, as Johnny Carson might say, some serious bondage stuff.

What we do offer, set against a playful backdrop of demons, tiny mad scientists, plesiosaurs, fairies, woodland creatures, and giant bees, is another heaping helping of impertinent lasses who, try as they may, just can't seem to slip the surly, but comparatively innocuous, bonds of F&L (and are, frankly, ever so much the better for it).

In addition, there's this little narrative fantasy called "The New Girl". It's Stantonesque, in the sense that our heroine is tied up, and things are done to her.

But there the similarities end. It's no **Evelyn Handleman in the Case of the V-Pants**, that's for sure.

Steve Fastner
Rich Larson
April, 2008

Rich Larson's
BED & BONDAGE
Volume Two

Book design by Grassy Knoll Studios.
Publishers: Sal Quartuccio and Bob Keenan
Published by
SQP Inc.
PO Box 248 - Columbus, NJ 08022

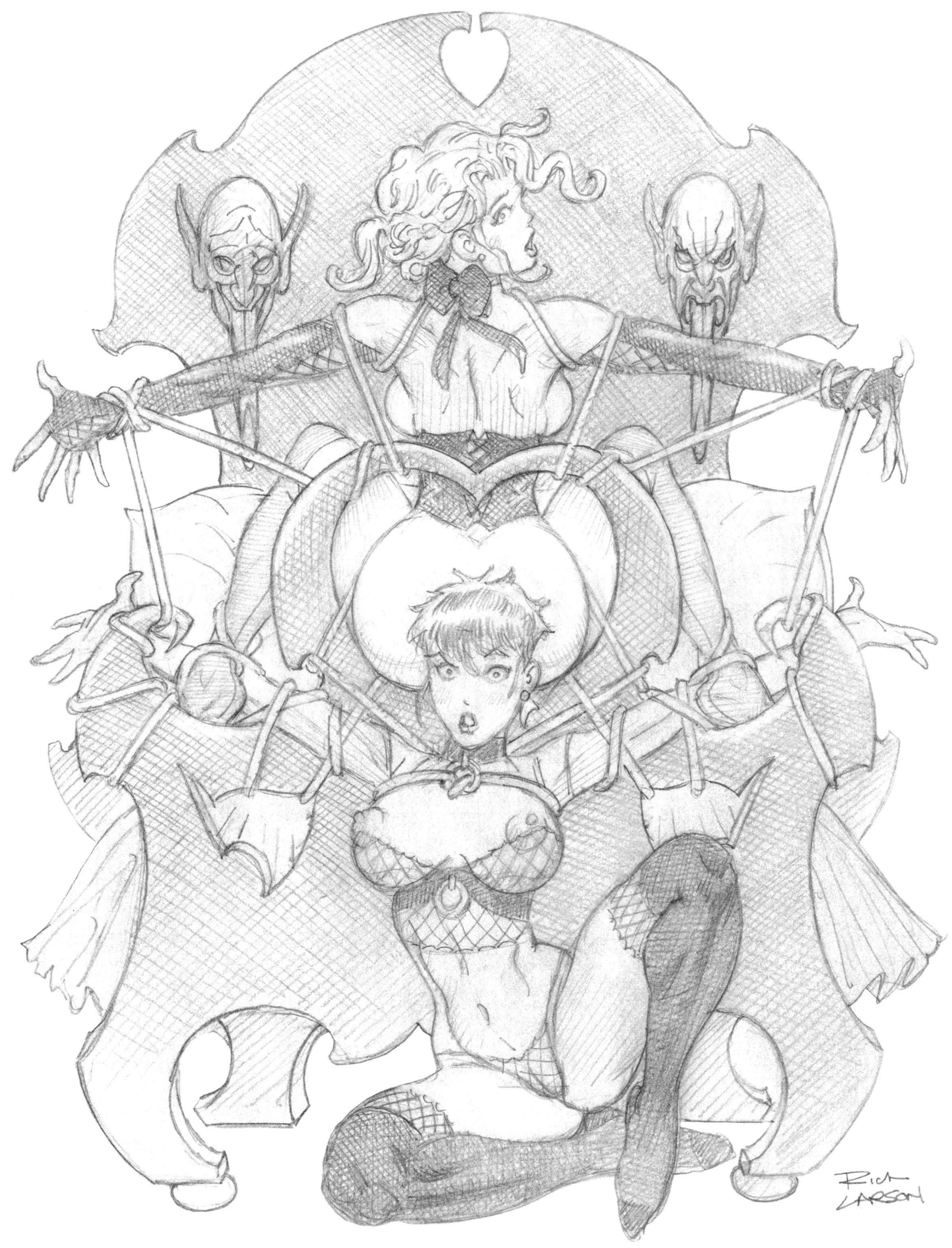

The Long Night

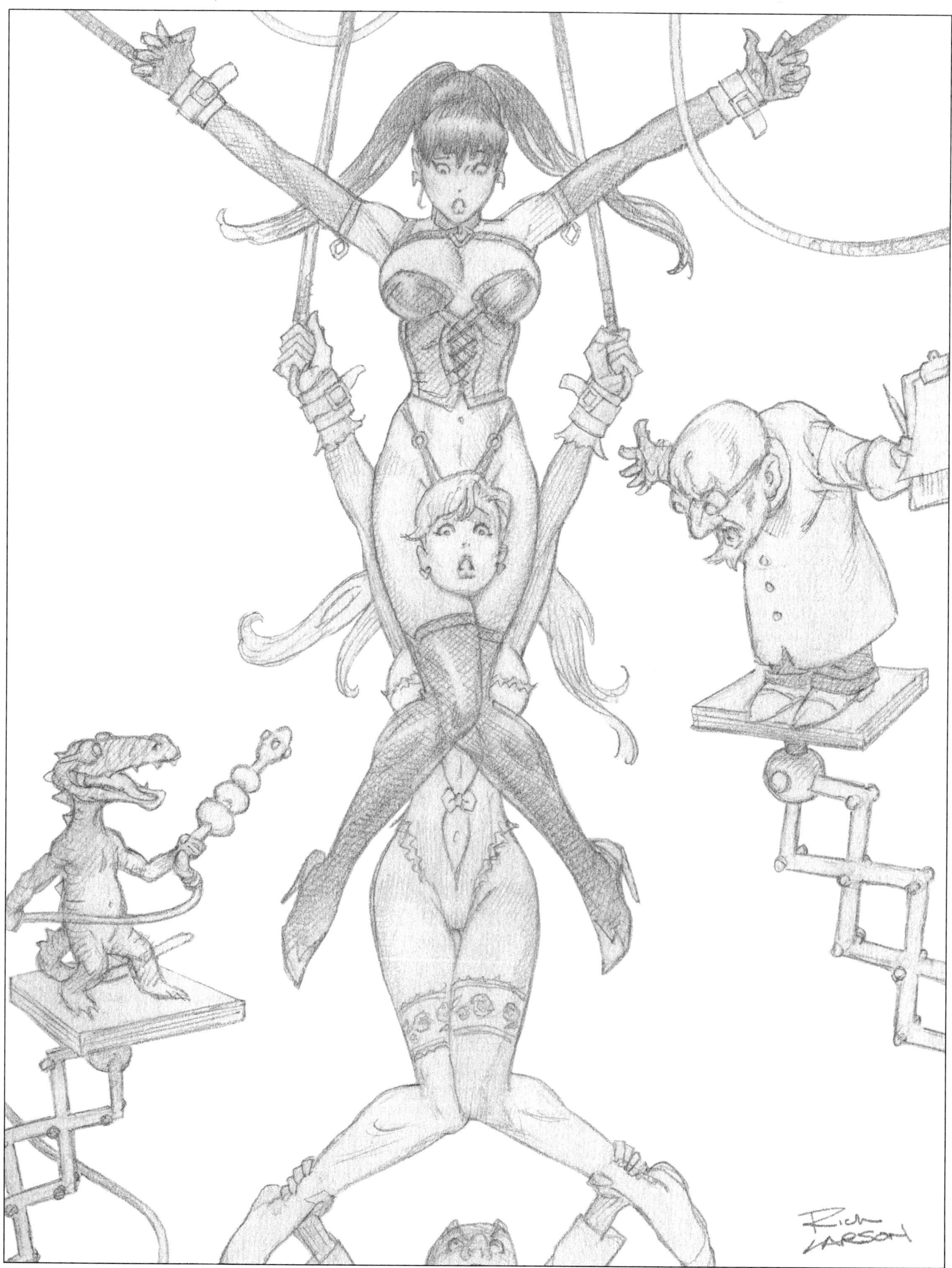

A Series of Tests

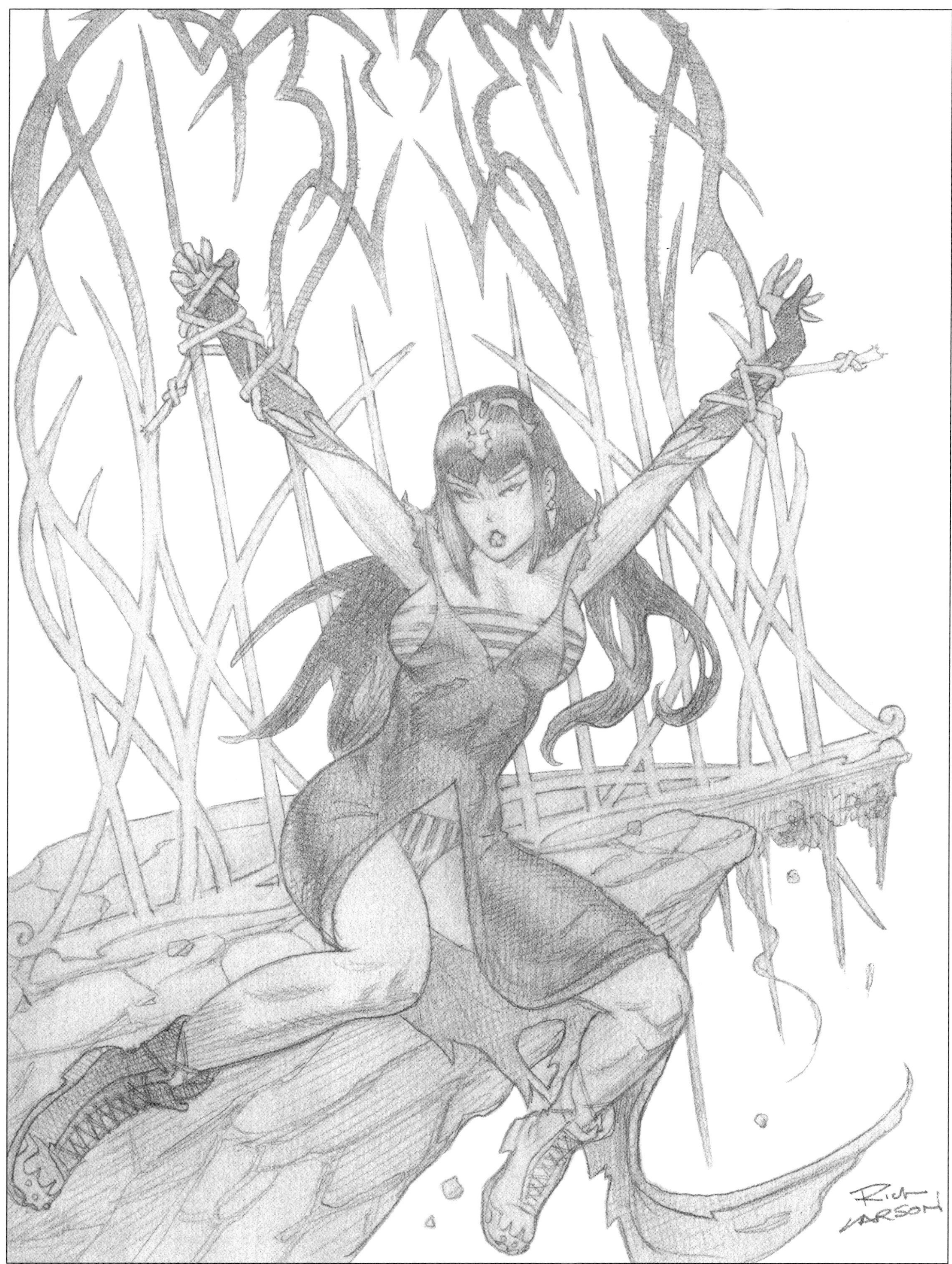

Black Siren

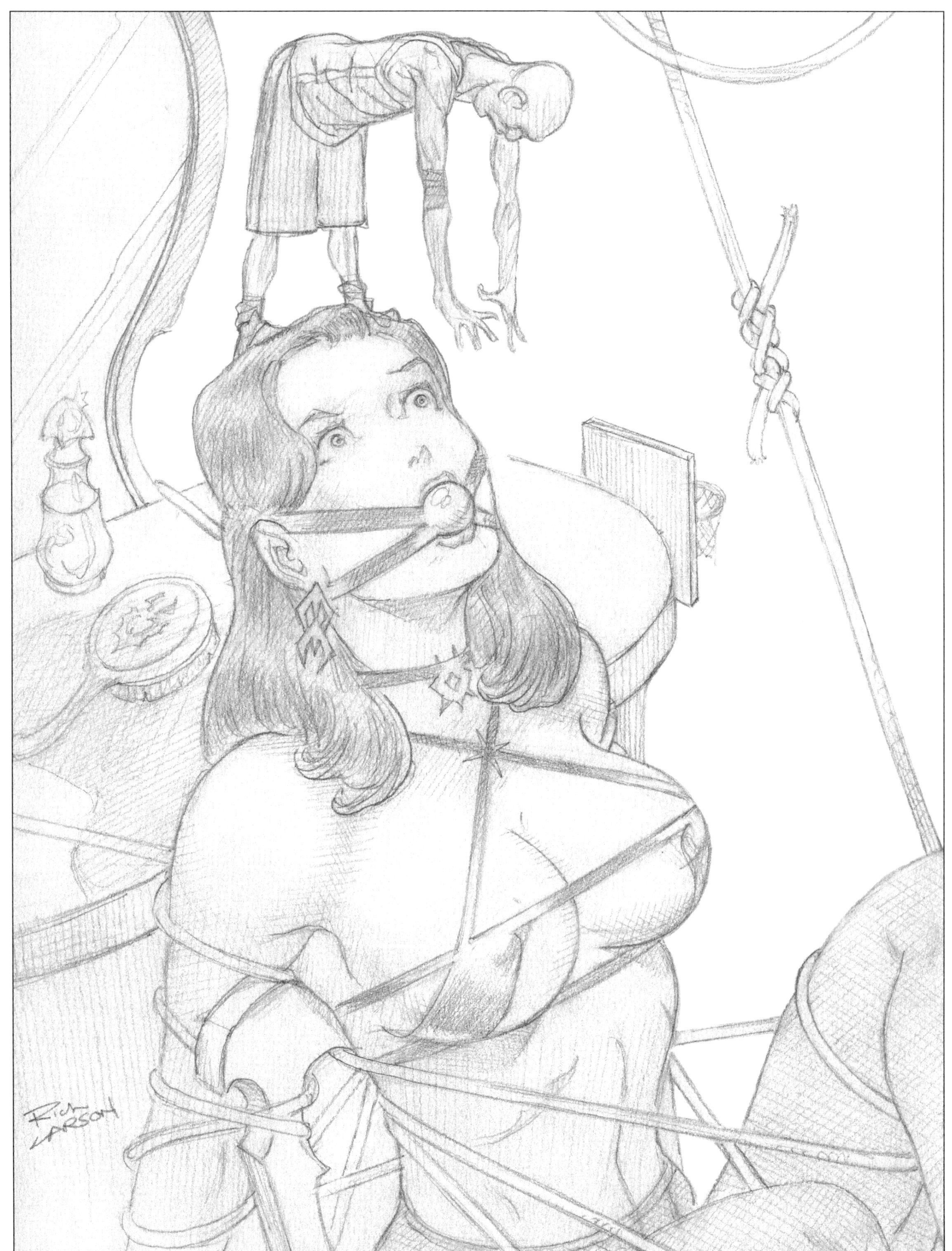

Game On

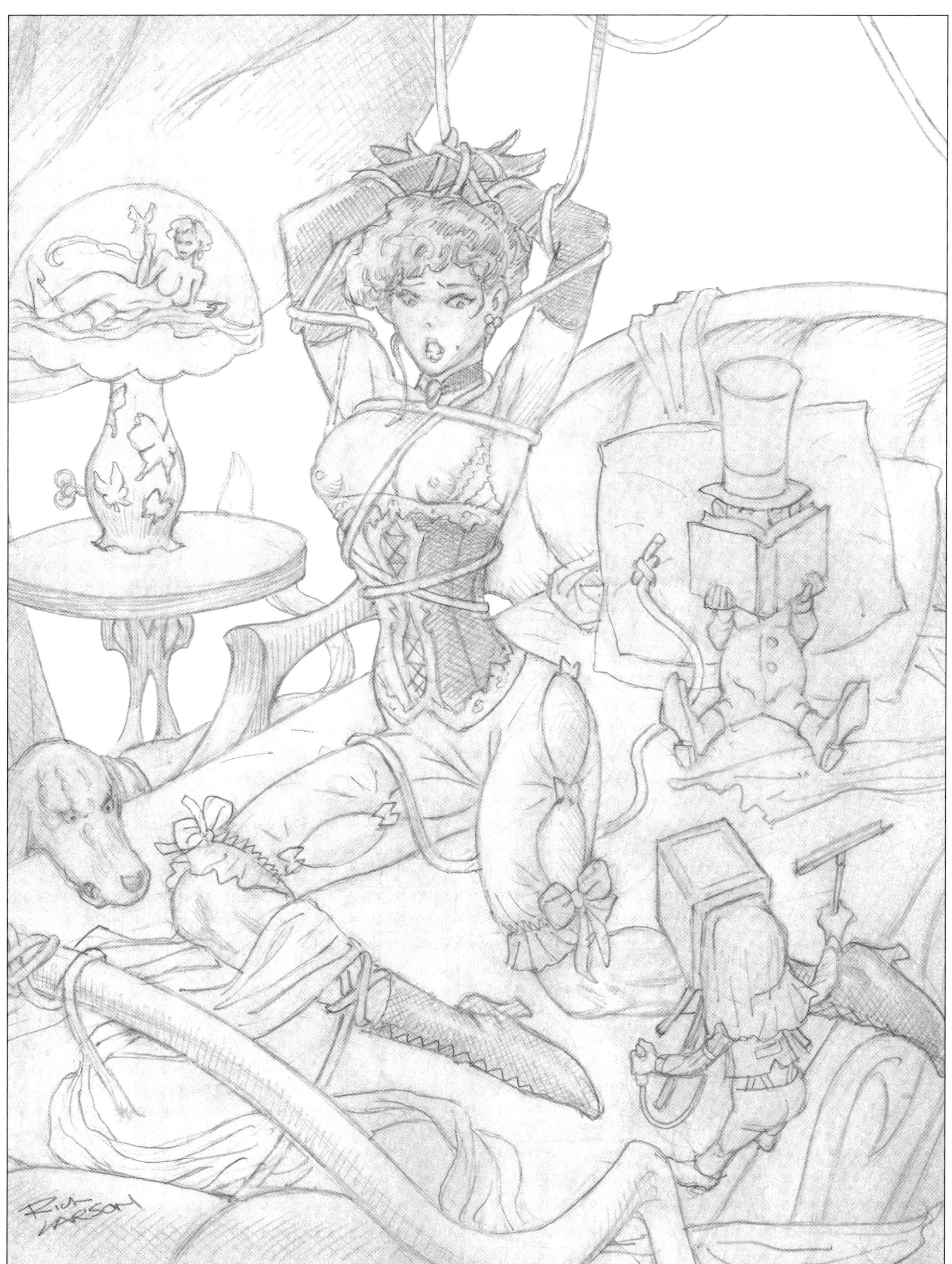

The New Pornographers

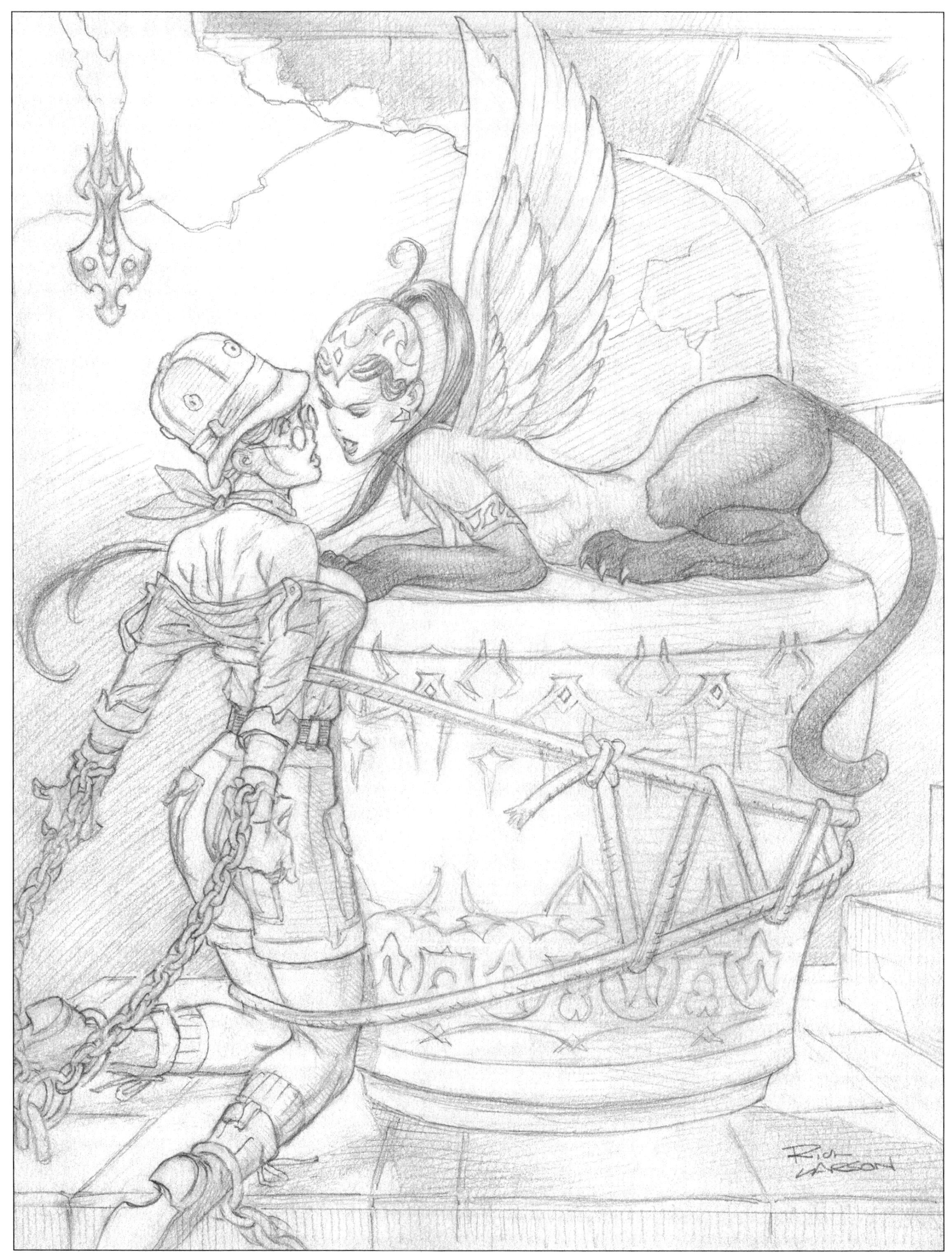

Baal In Heat

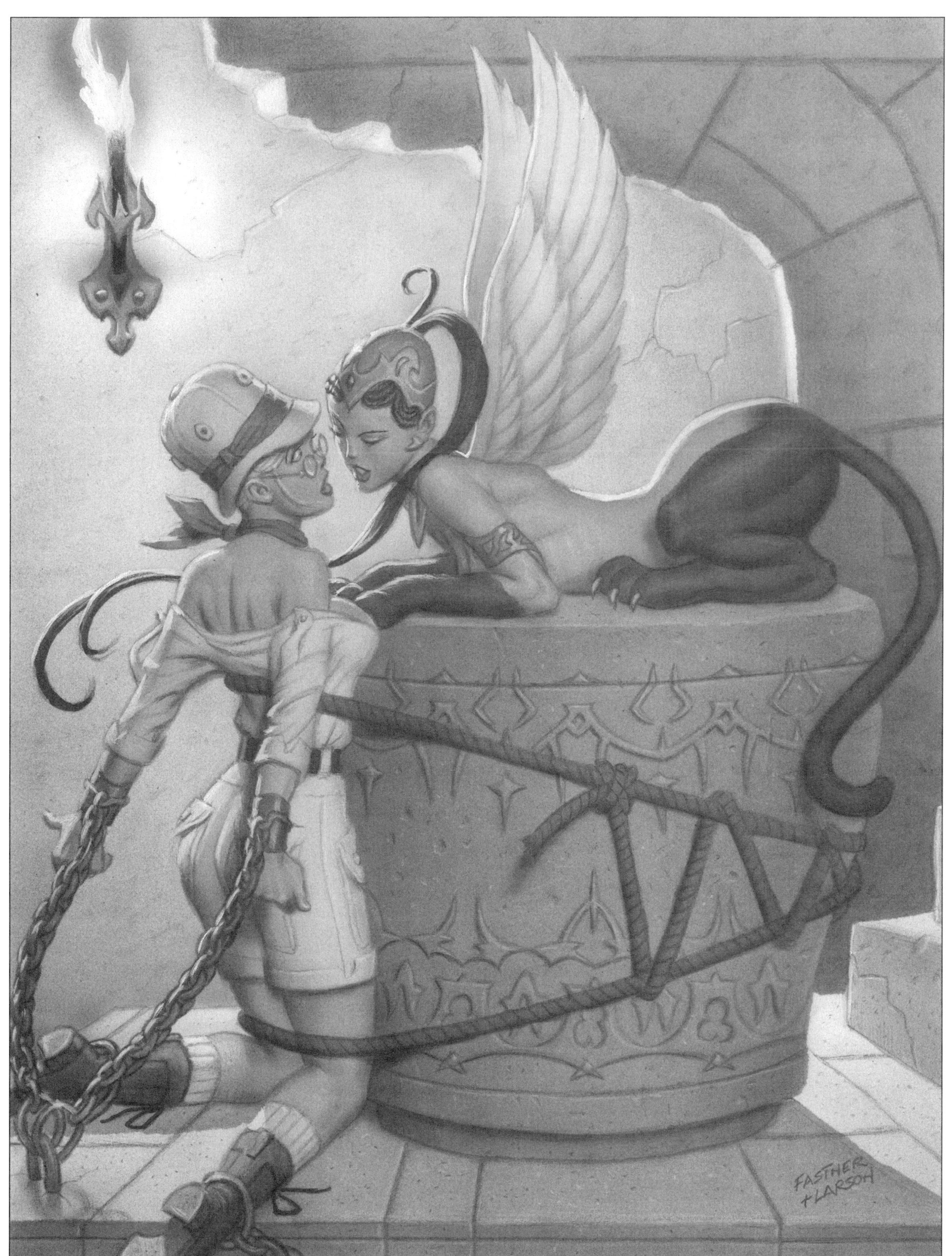

Baal In Heat - Painting

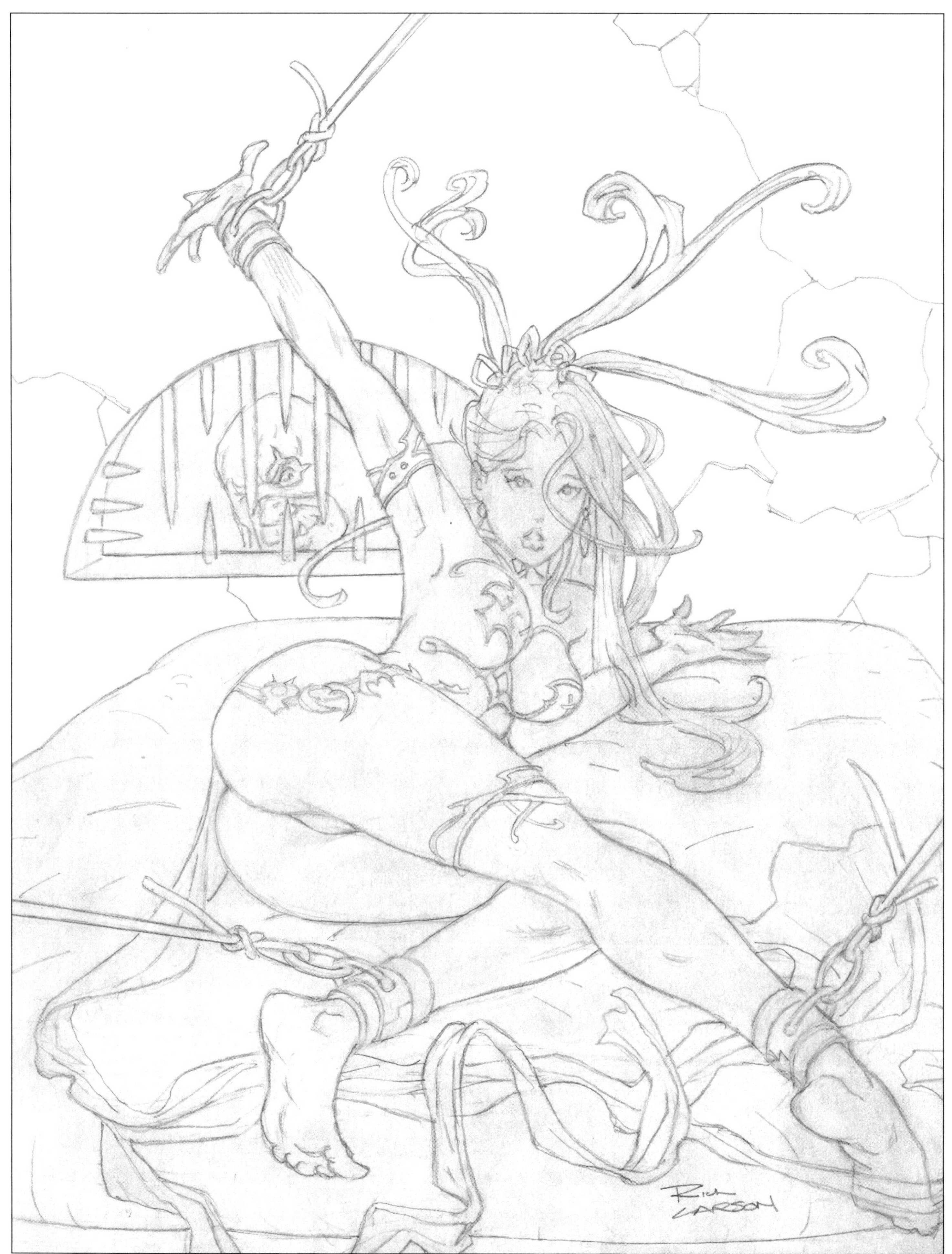

Caged Heat

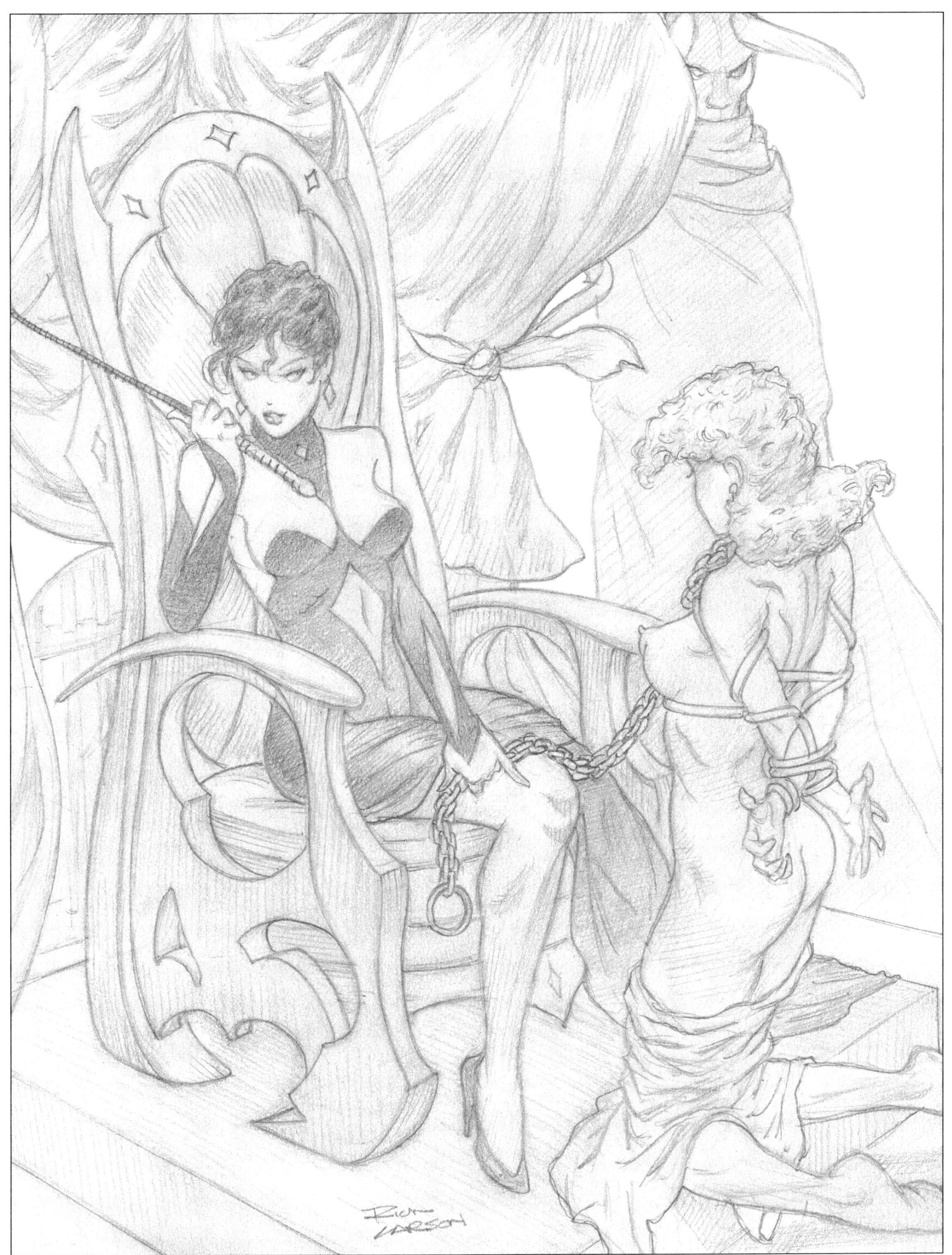

The Once Over

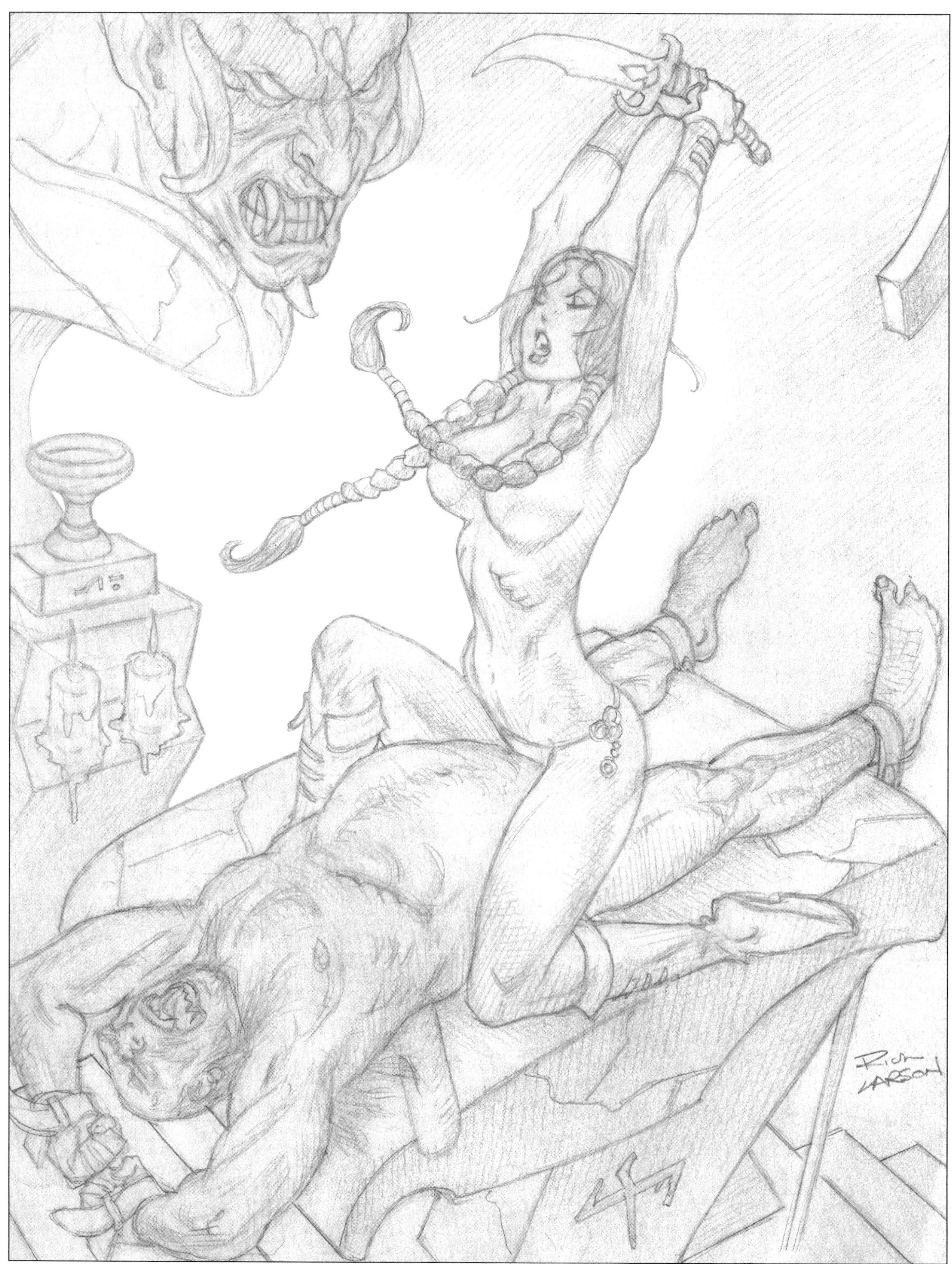

There Will Be Blood

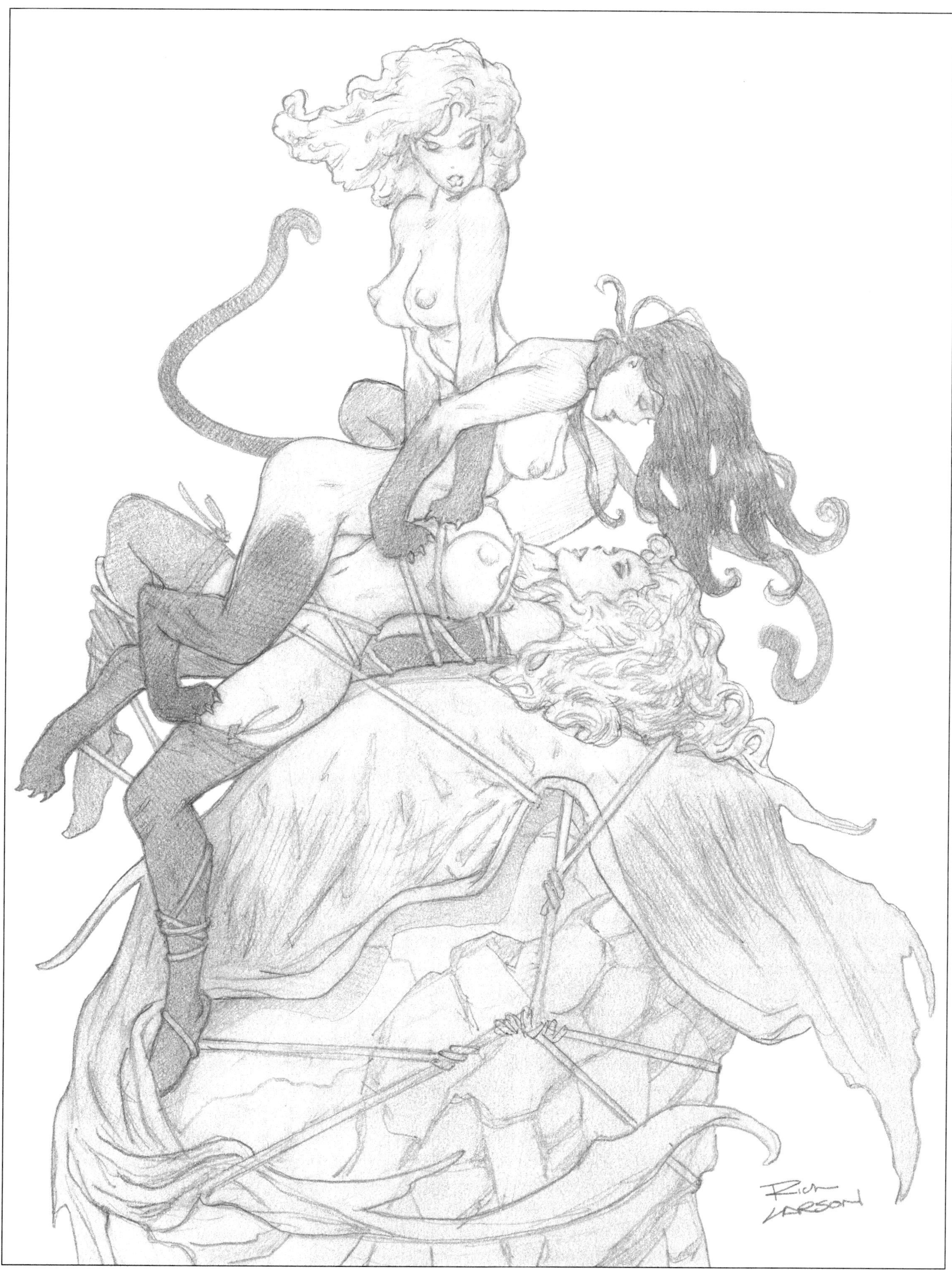

Pawed

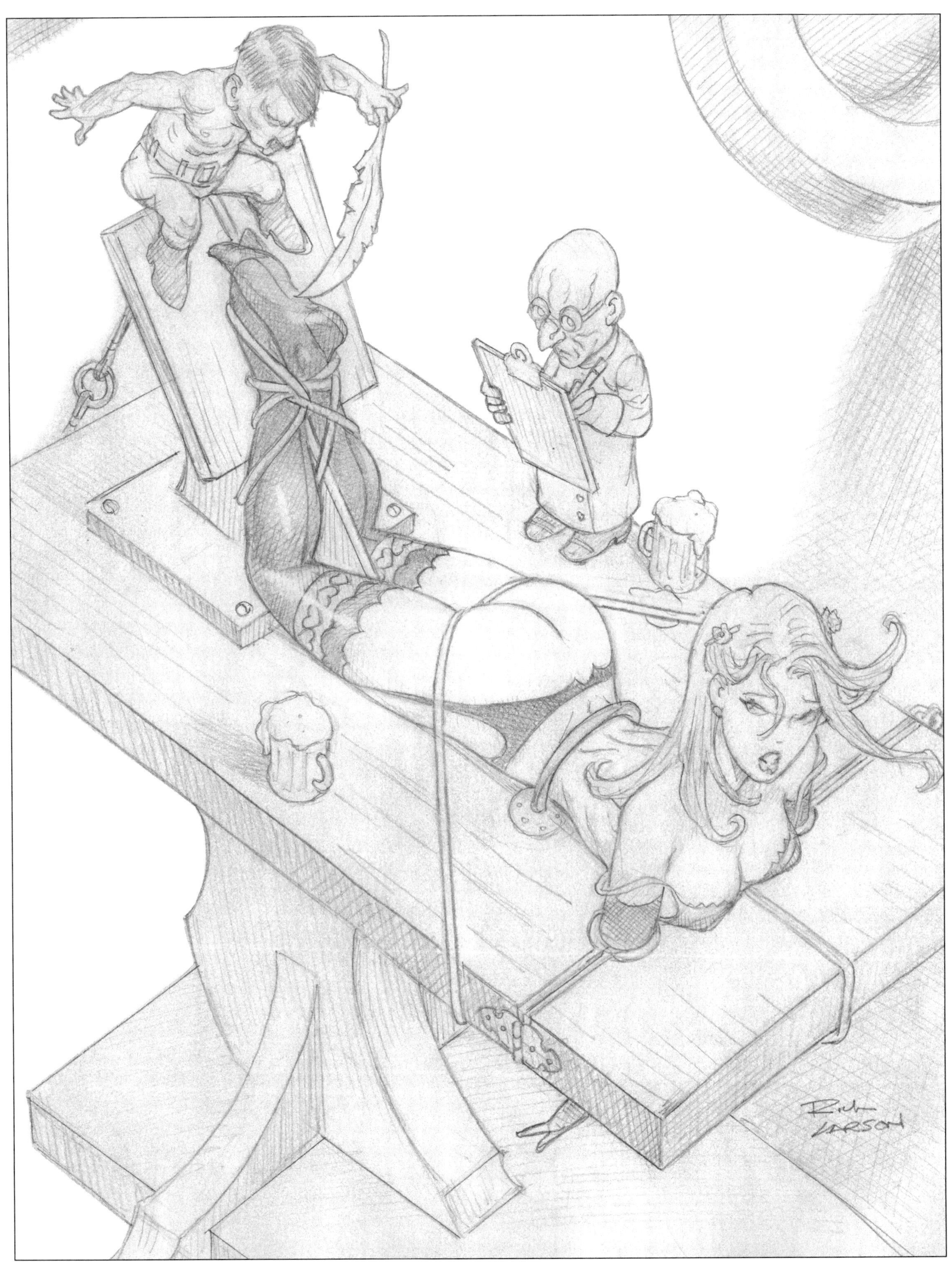

Busman's Holiday

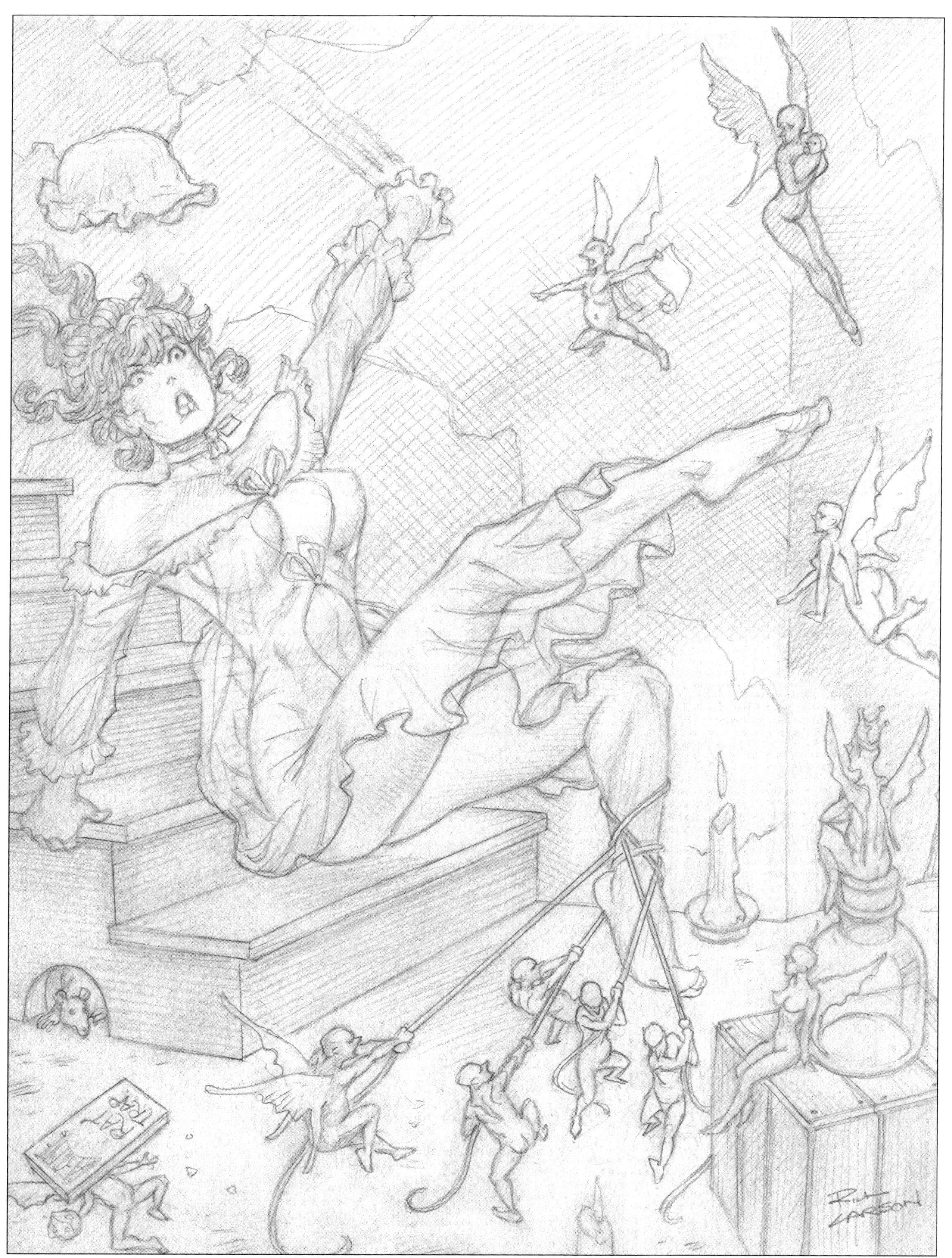

Audience With The King

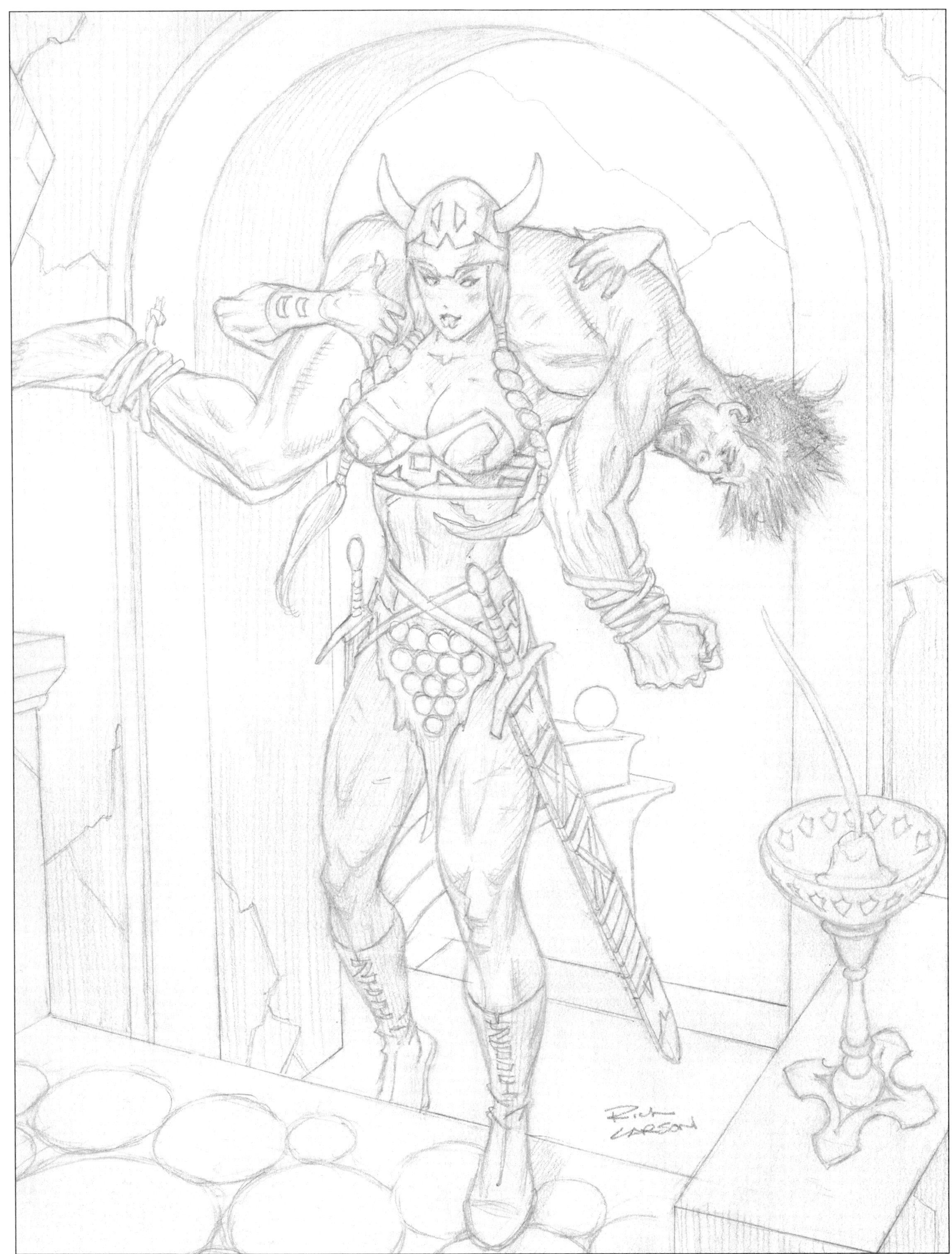

First Date

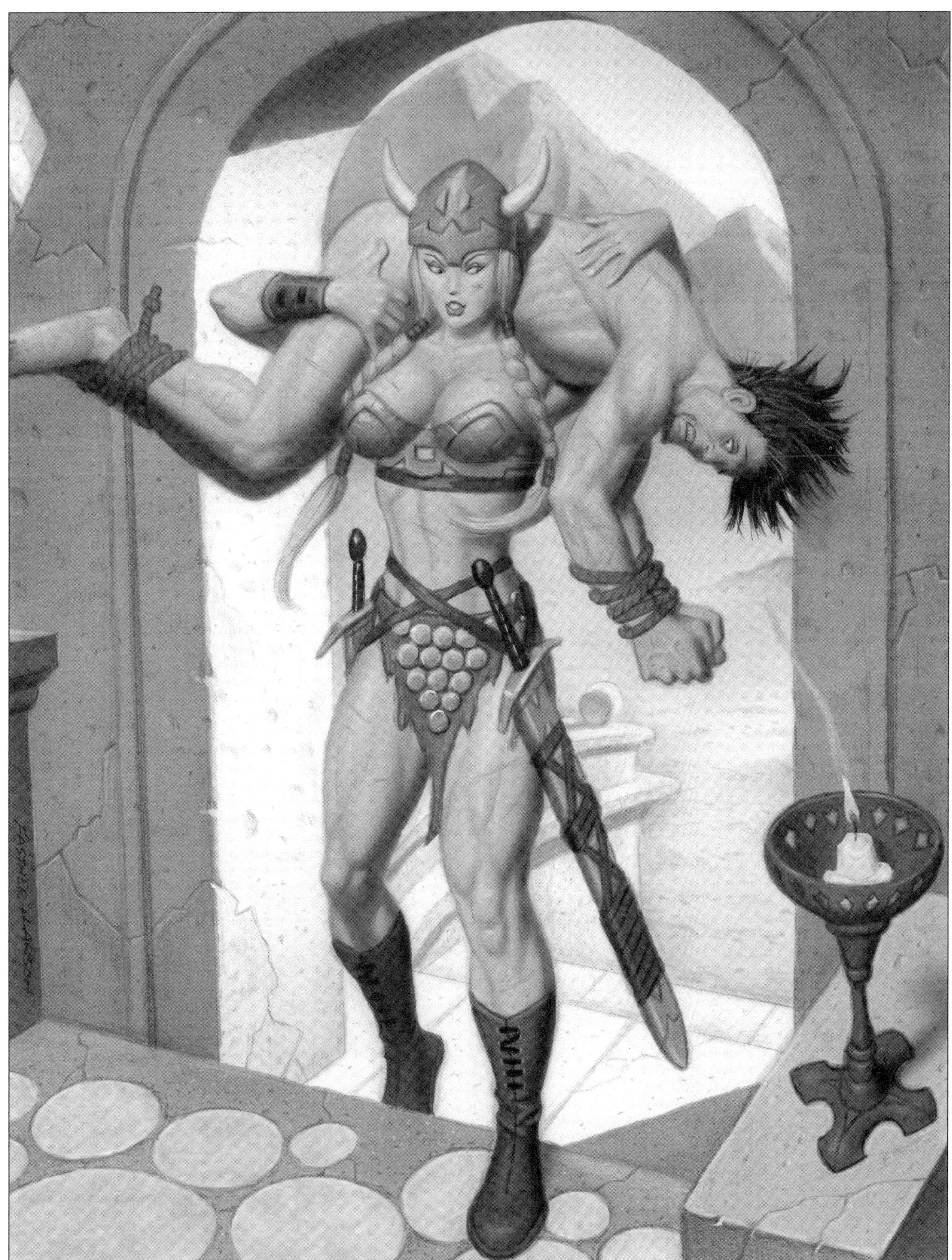

First Date - Painting

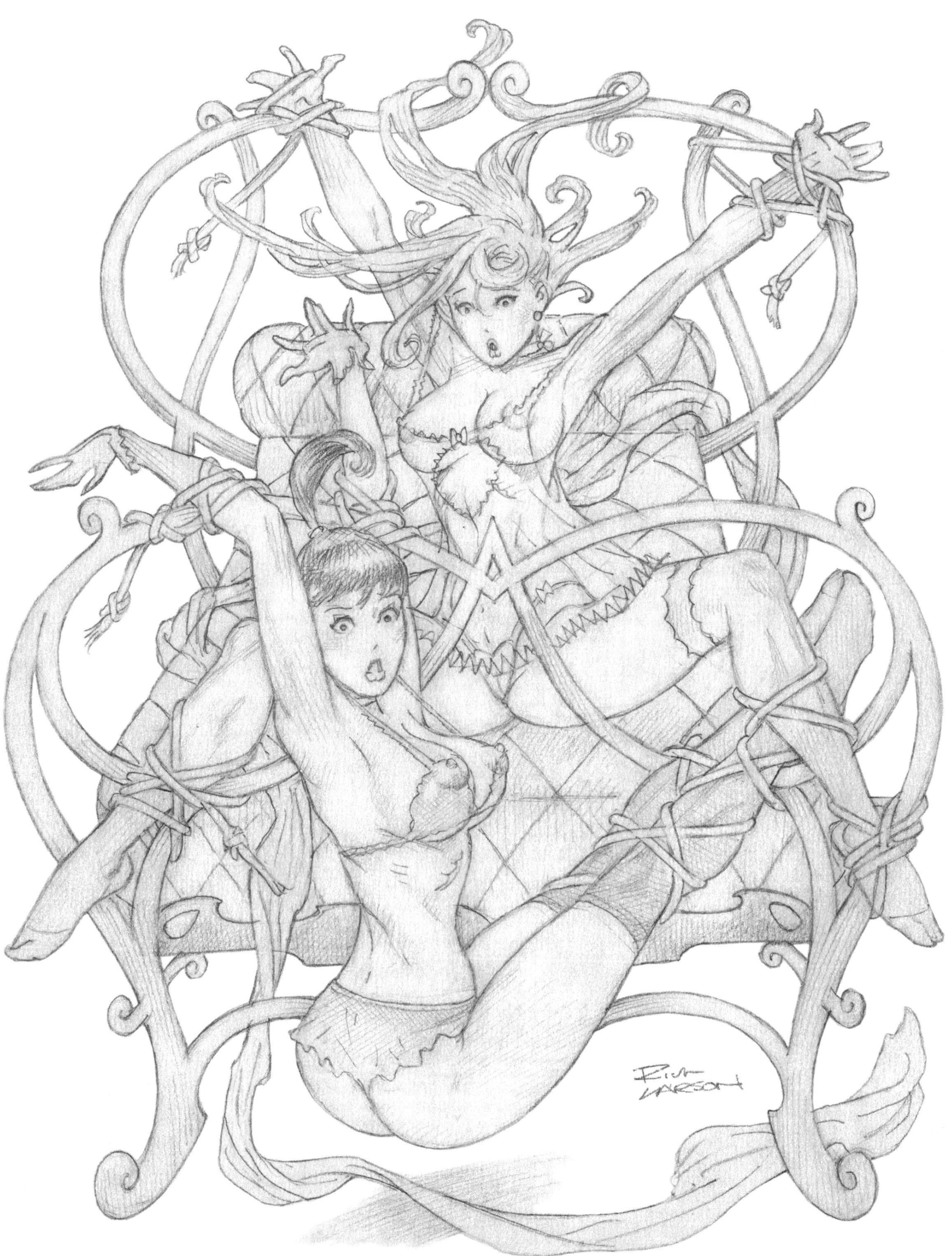

Over Wrought Iron

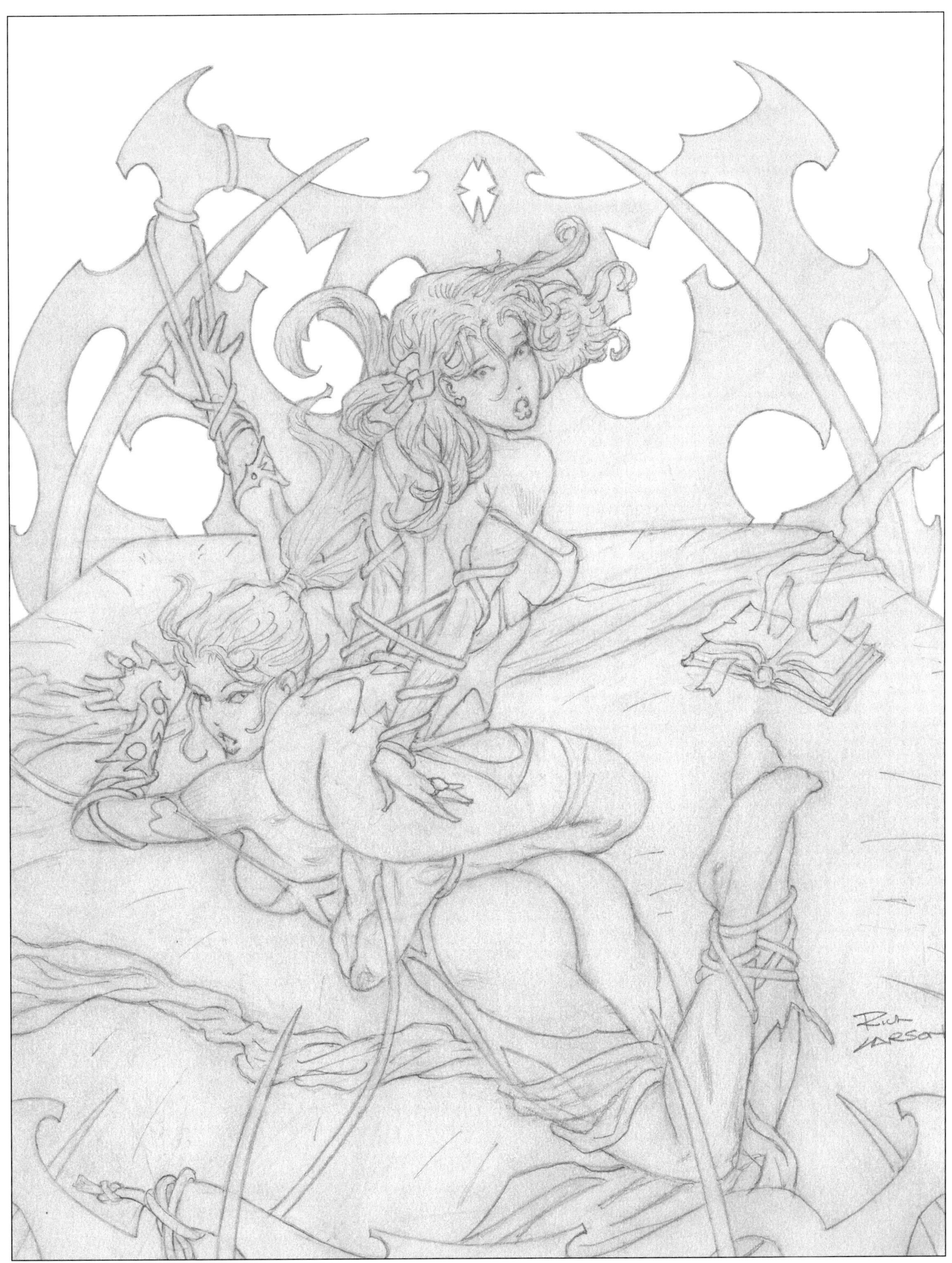

Book Of Dreams

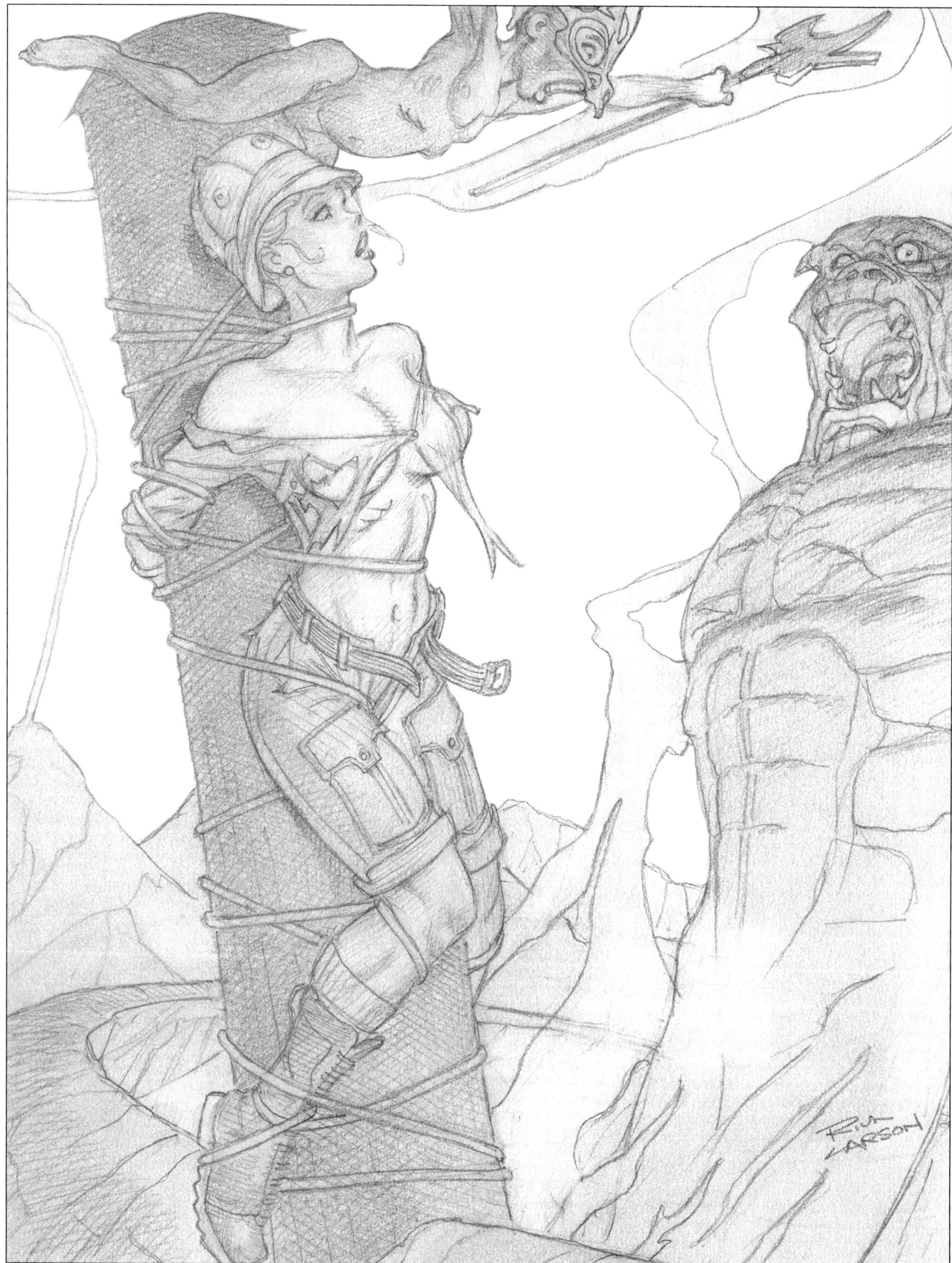

Shoo!

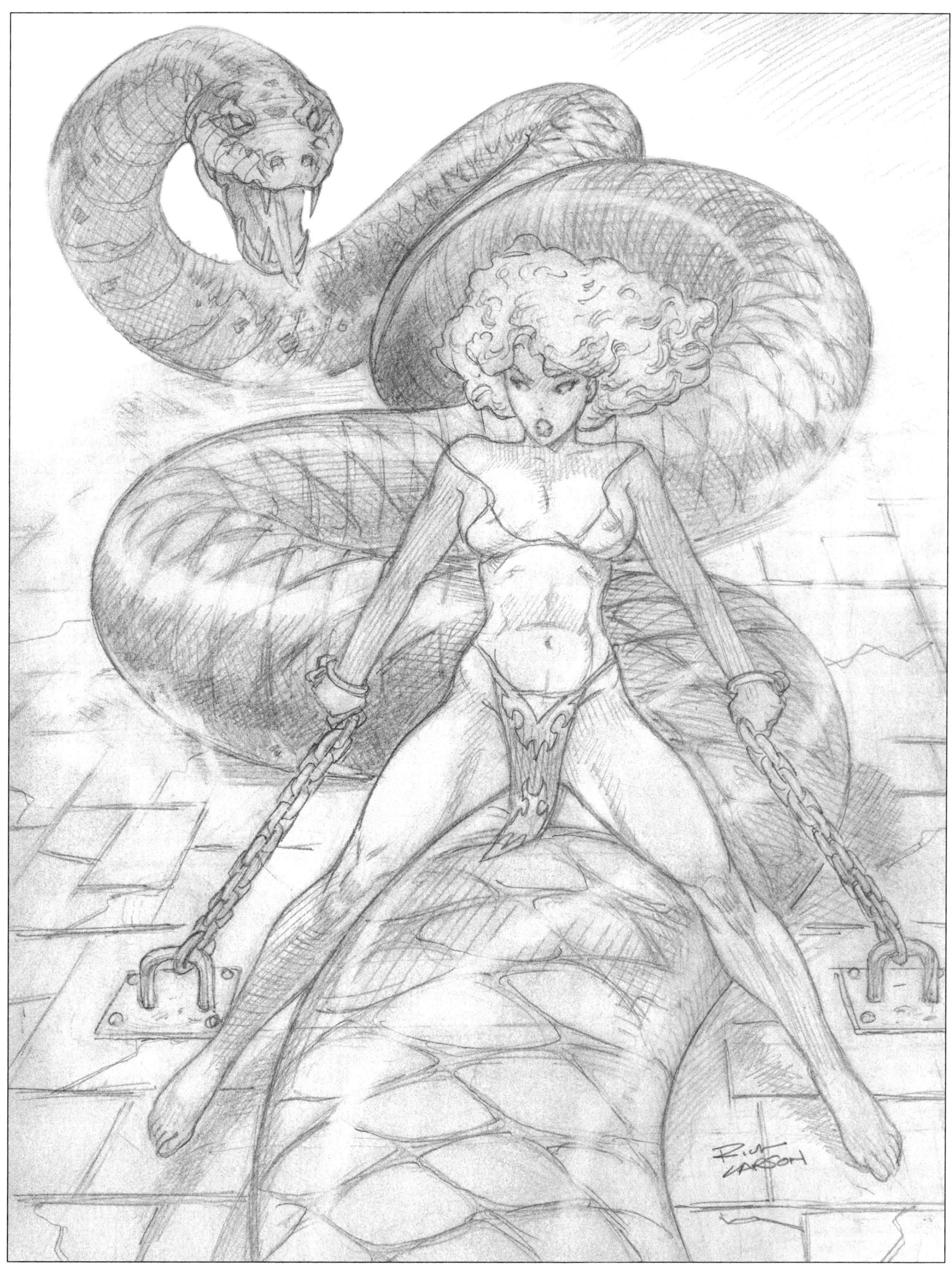

Scales of Doom

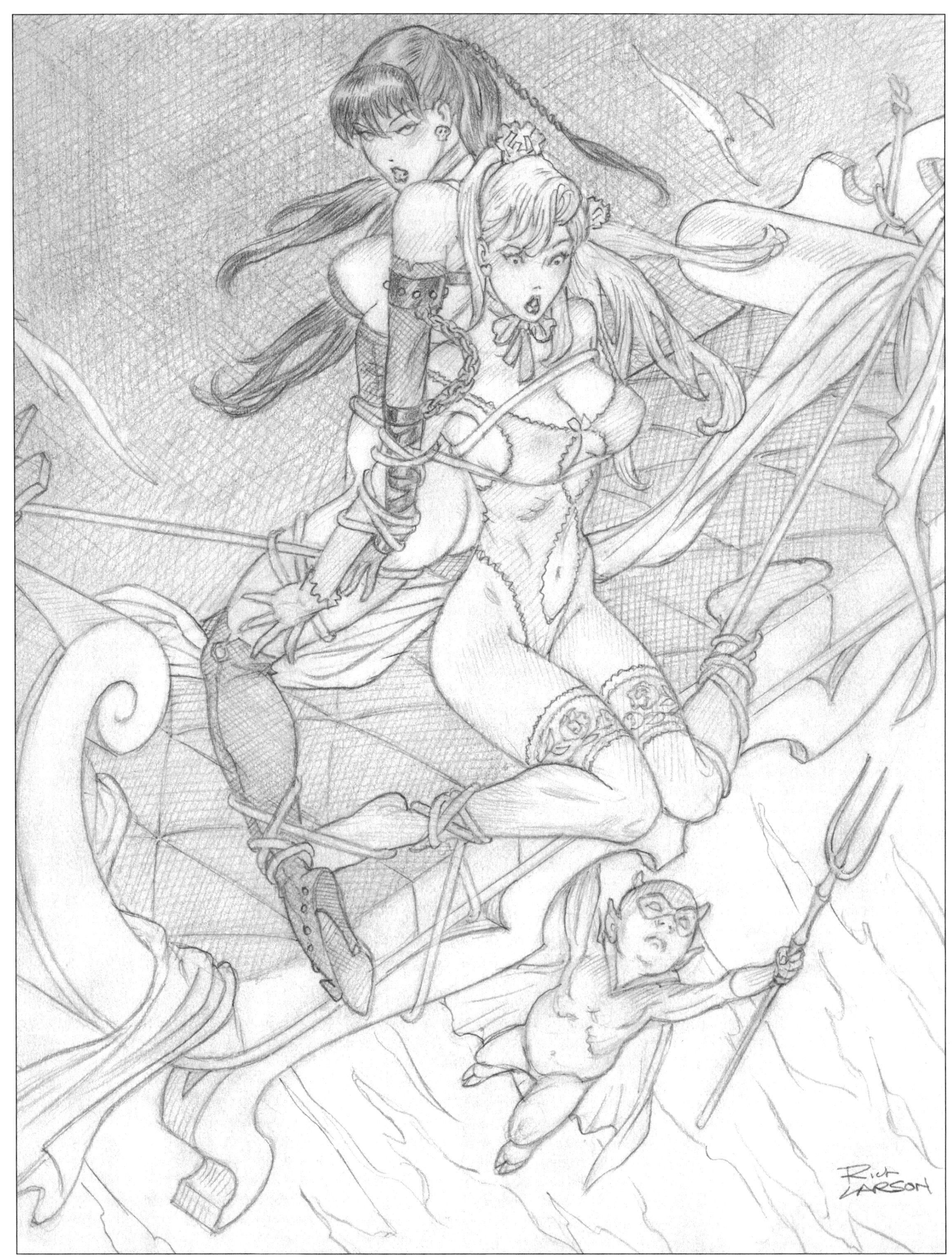

Something They Ate

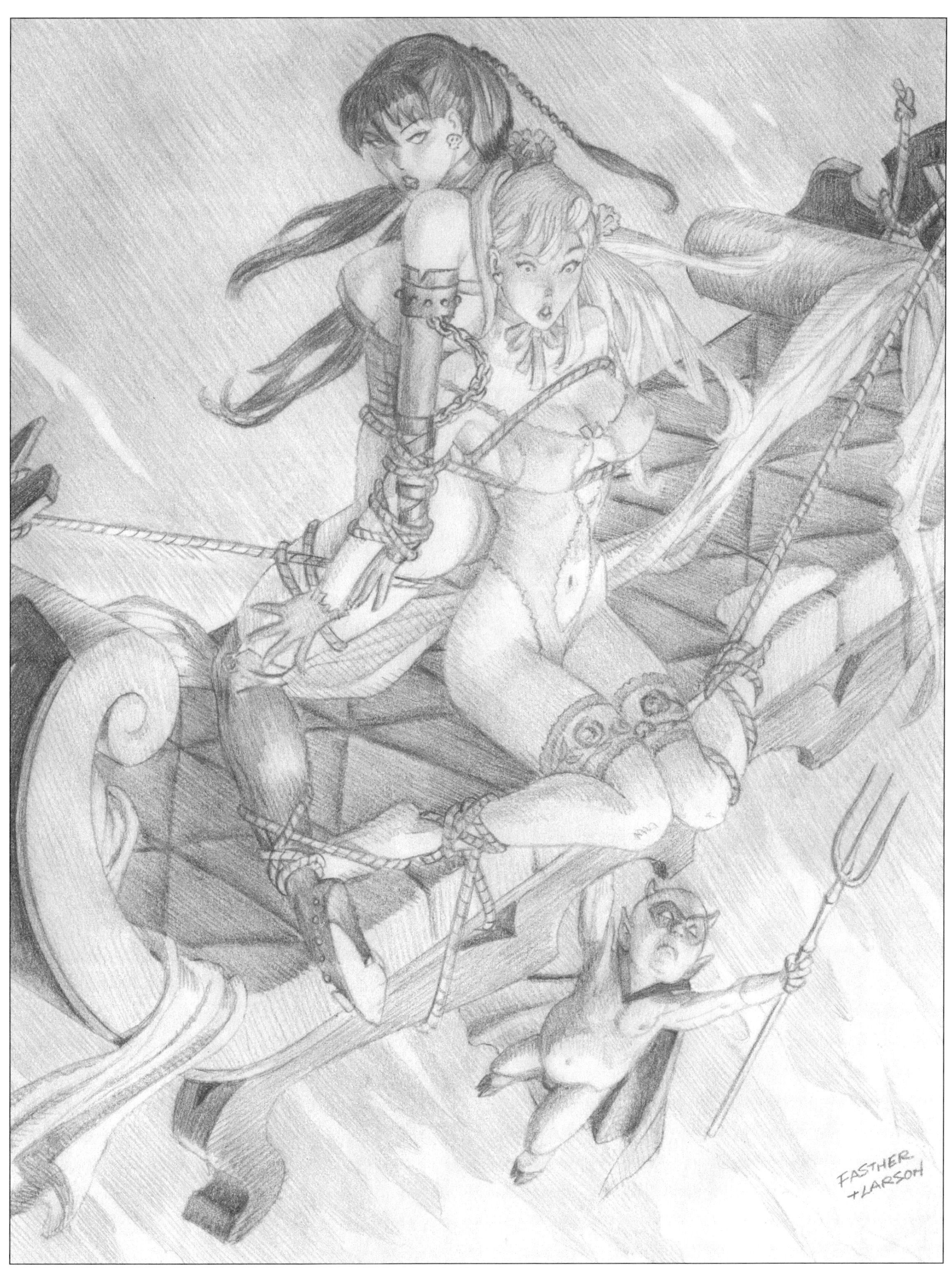

Something They Ate - Toned

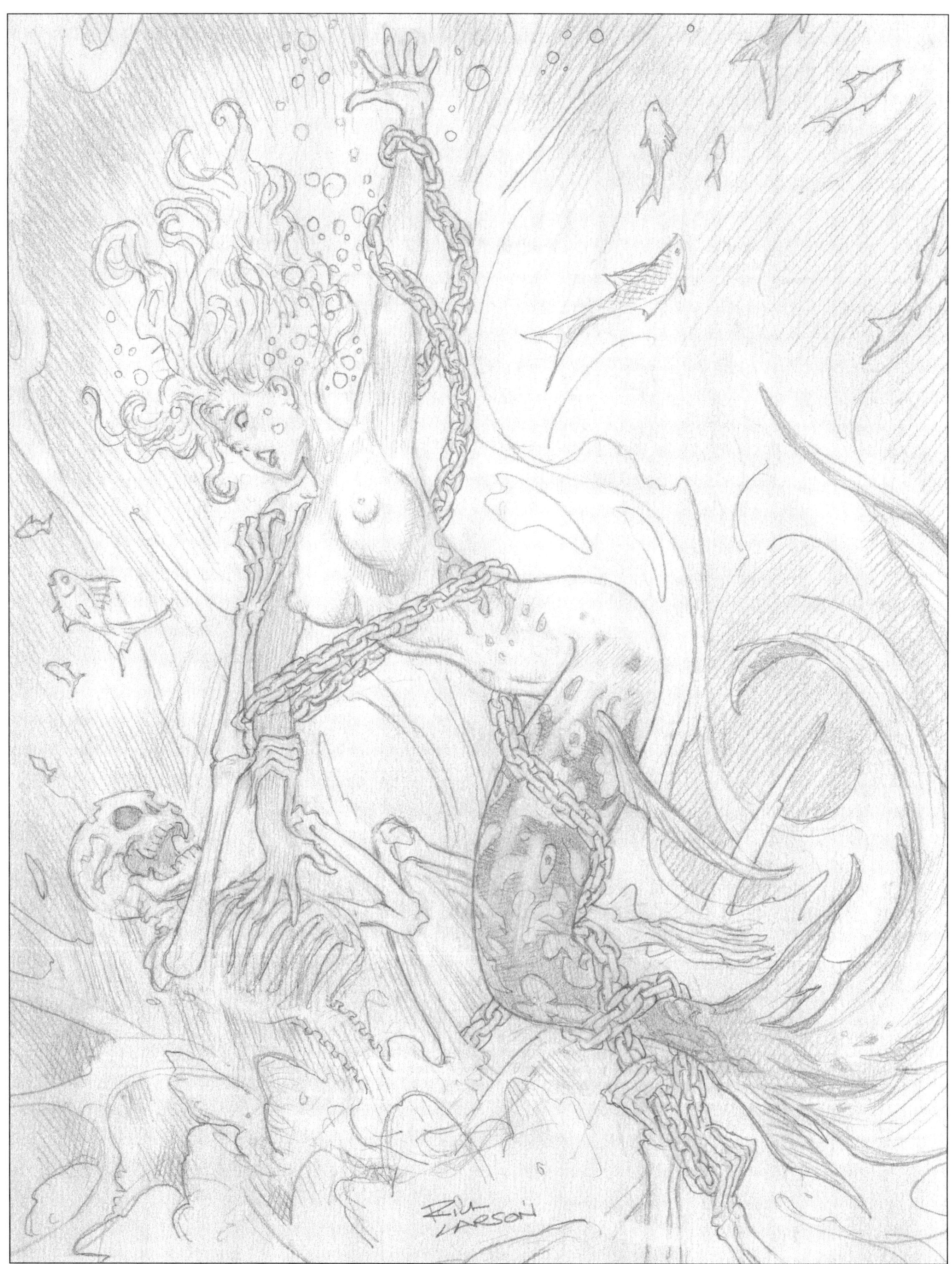

Deep Sixed

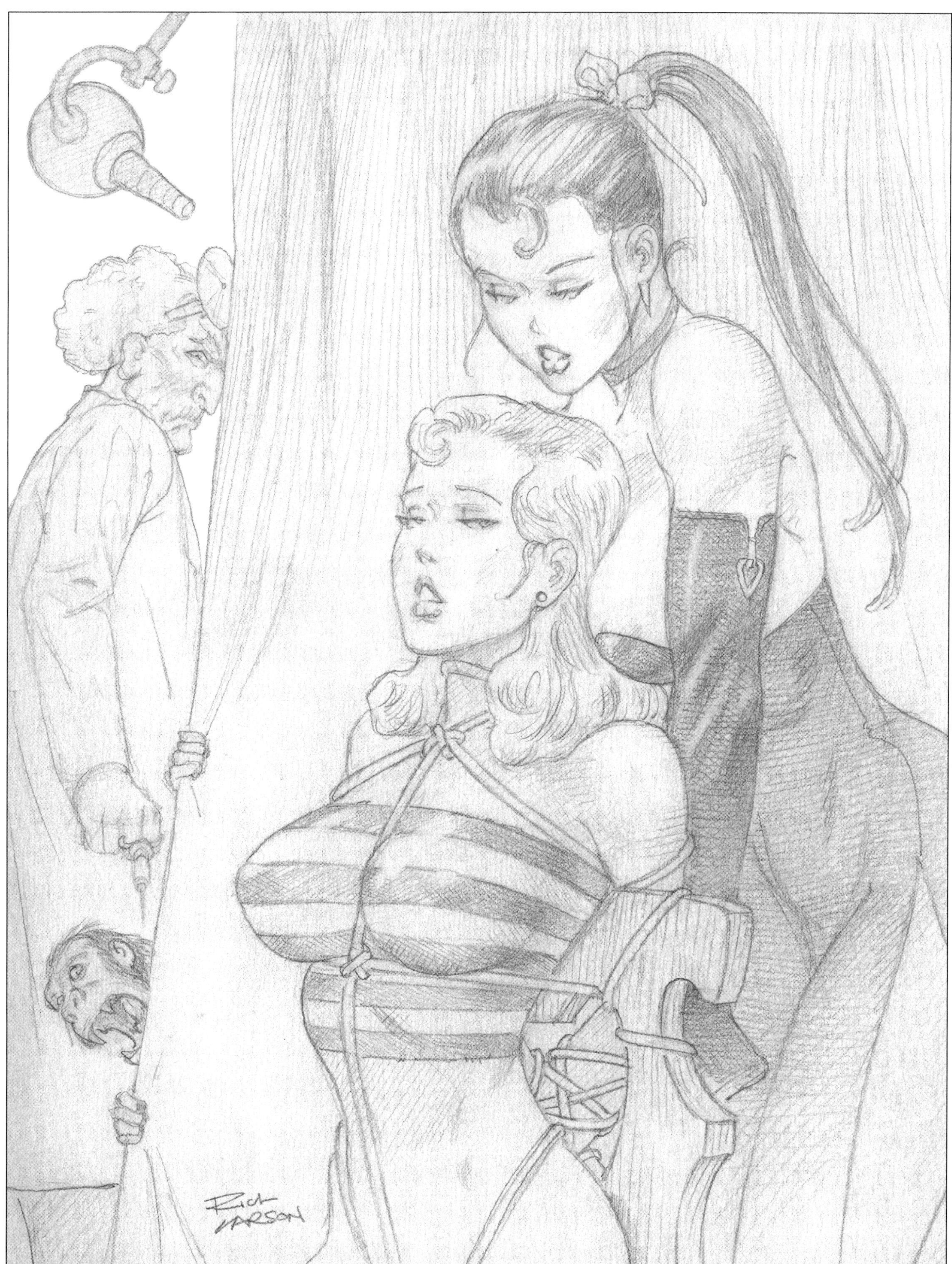

Love Doctor

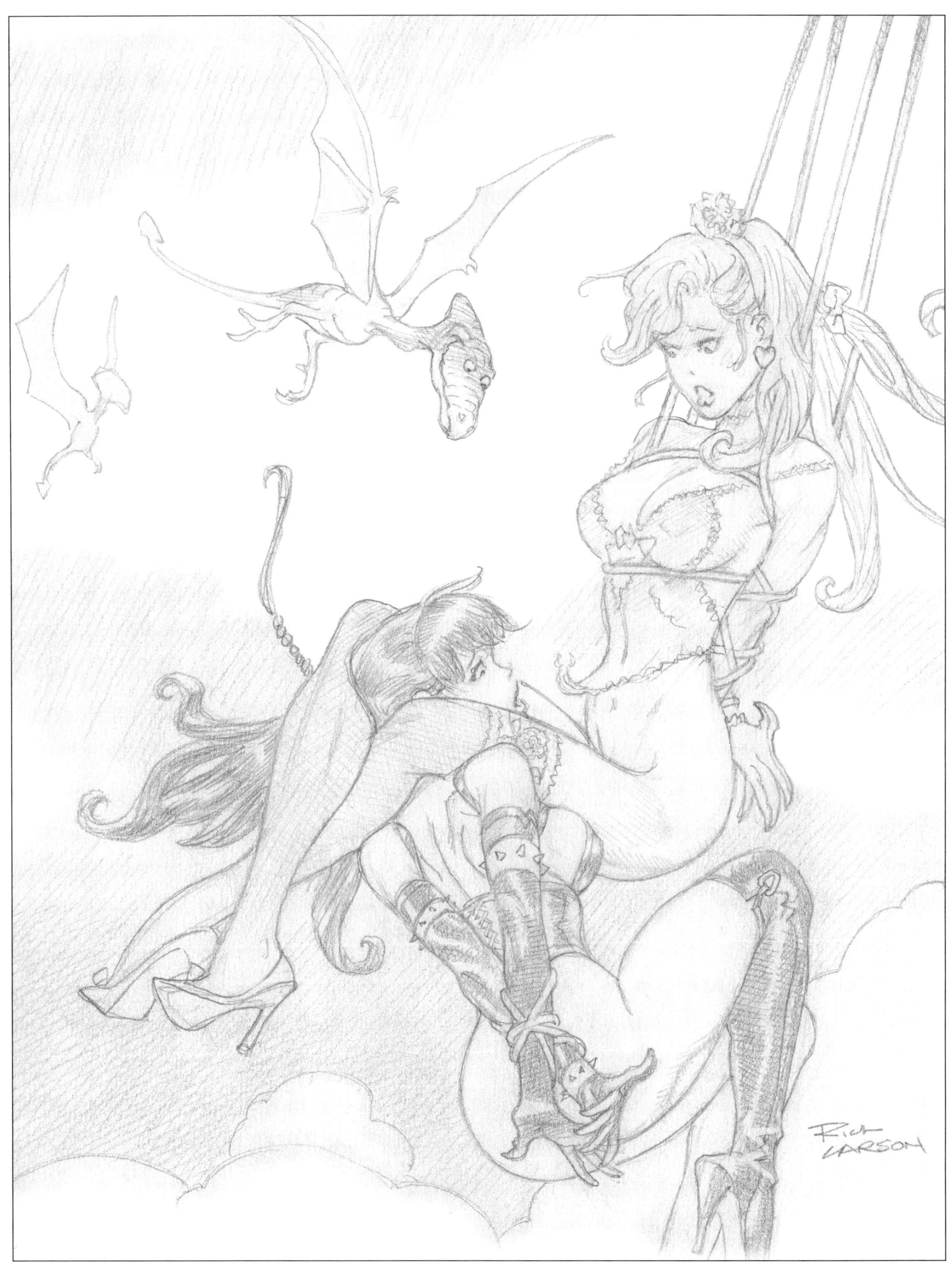

Hold on Tight

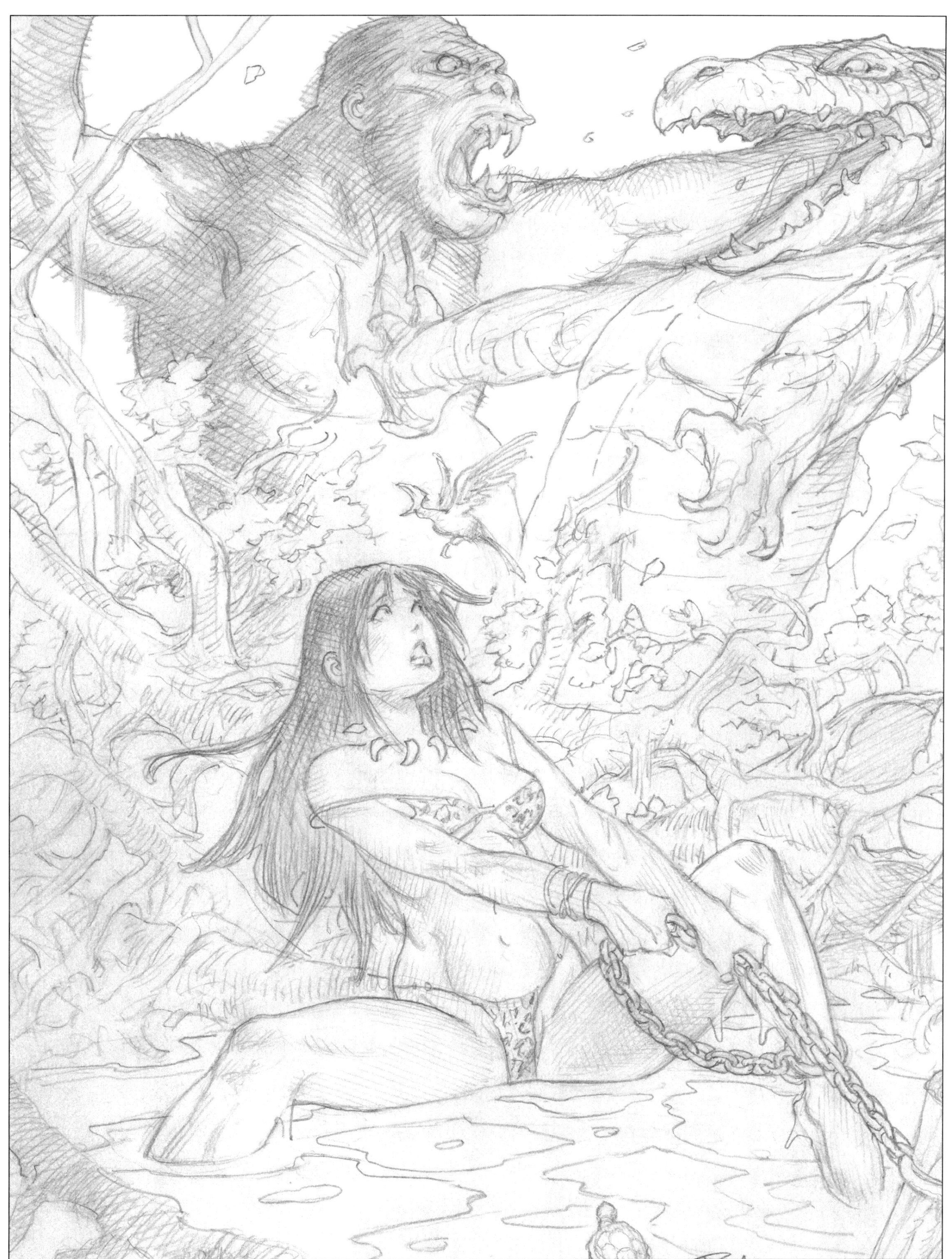

Neighborhood Squabble

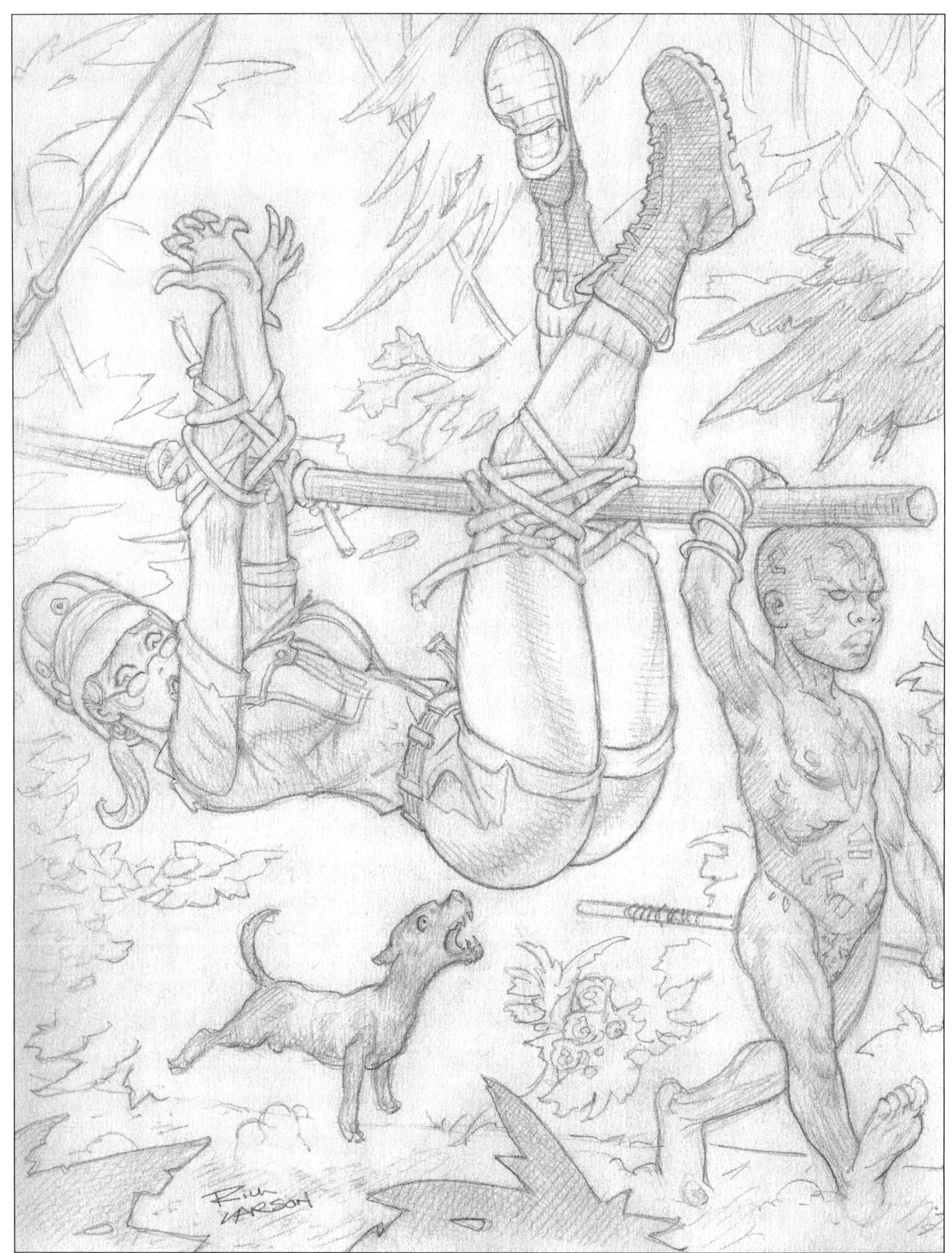

The Impossible Dream

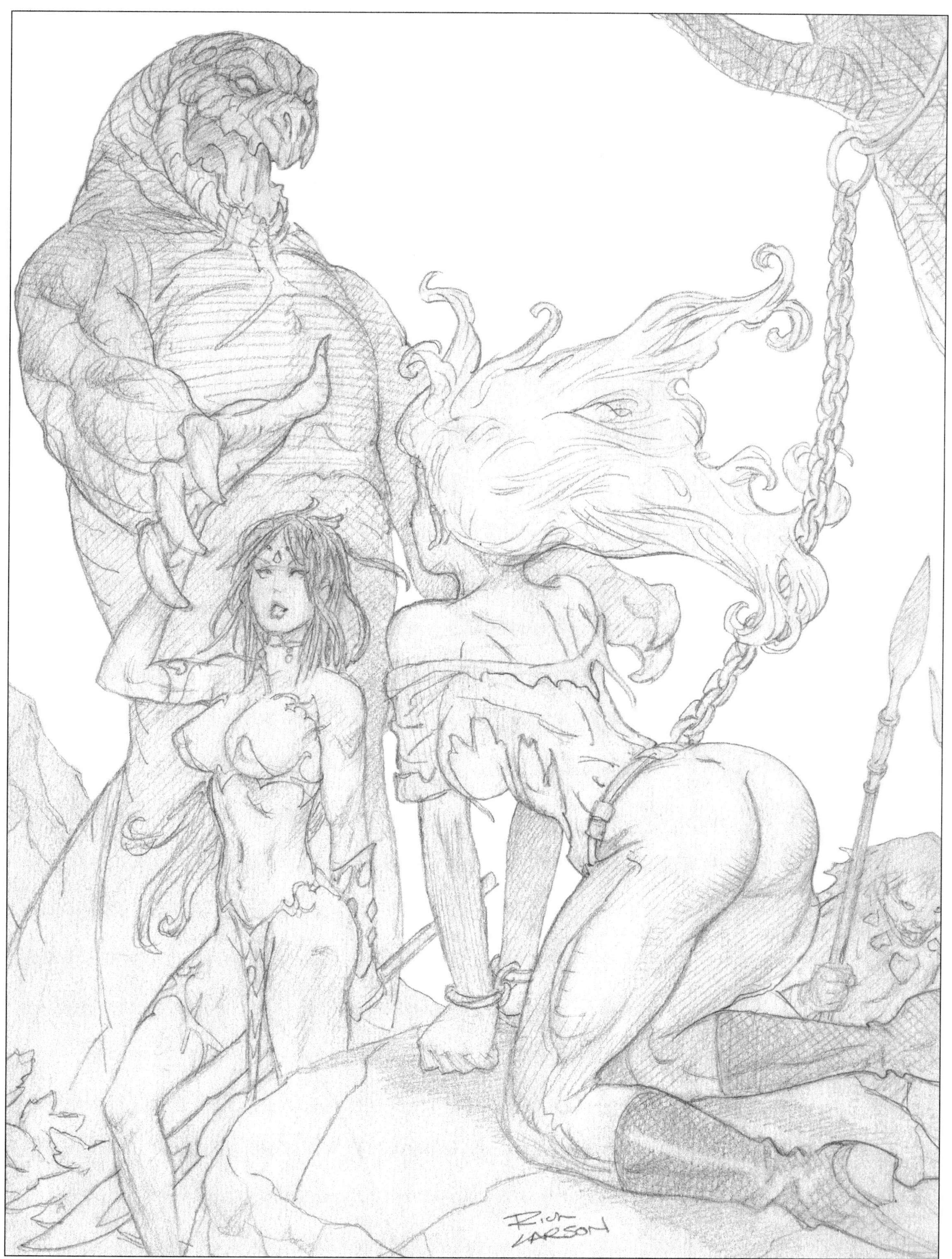

Take Her, She's Mine

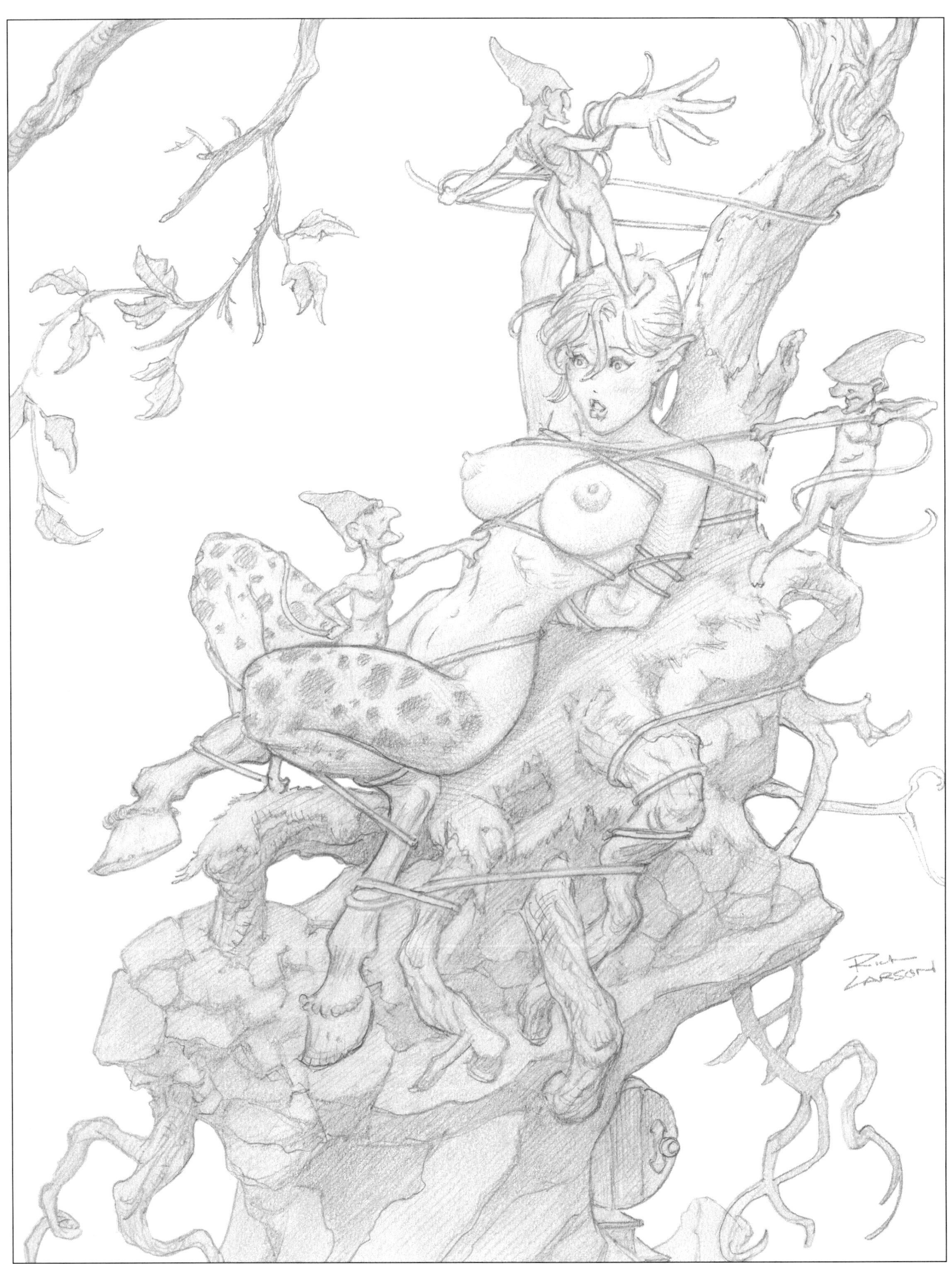

Wrong Place for a Nap

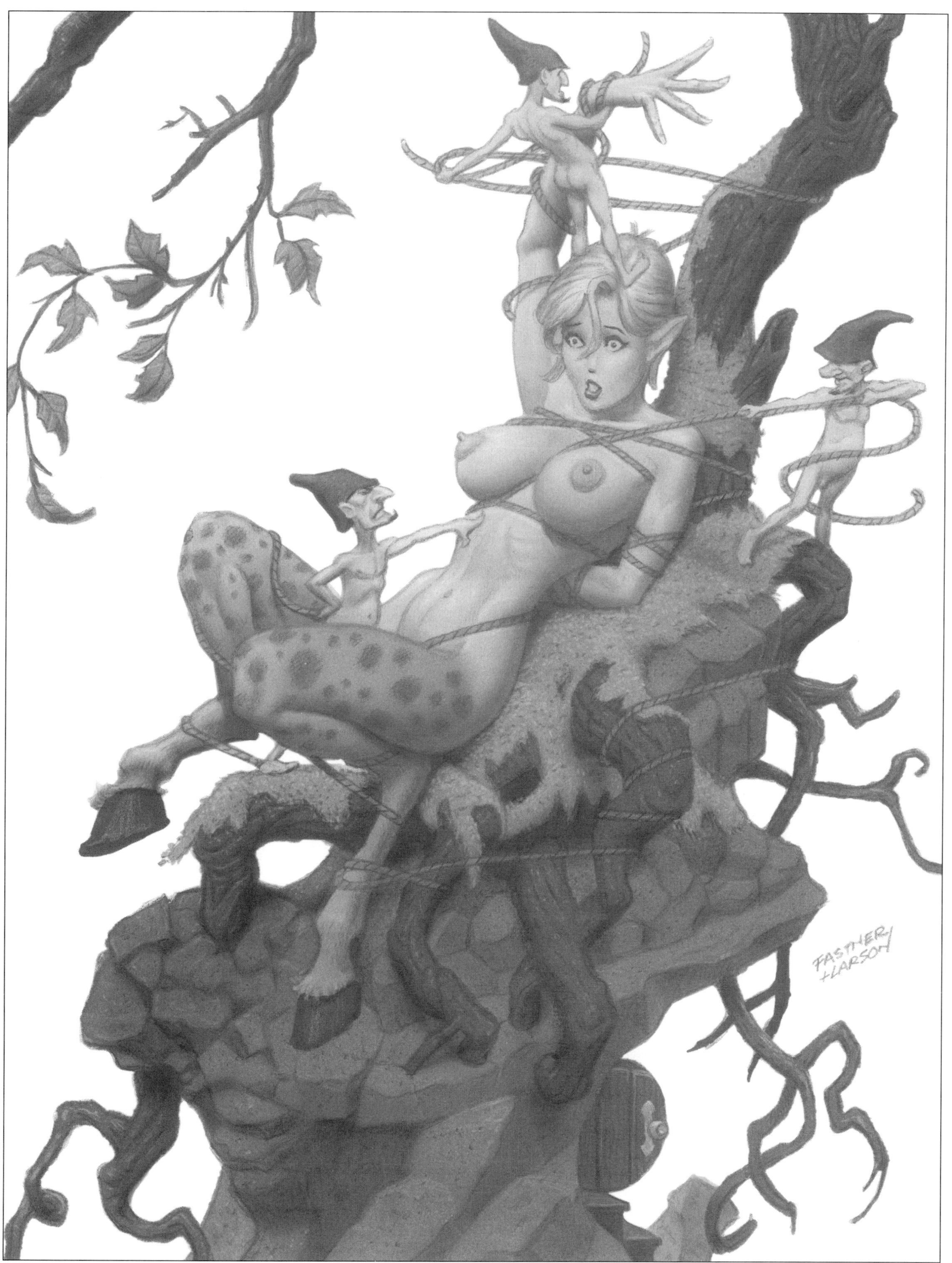

Wrong Place for a Nap - Painting

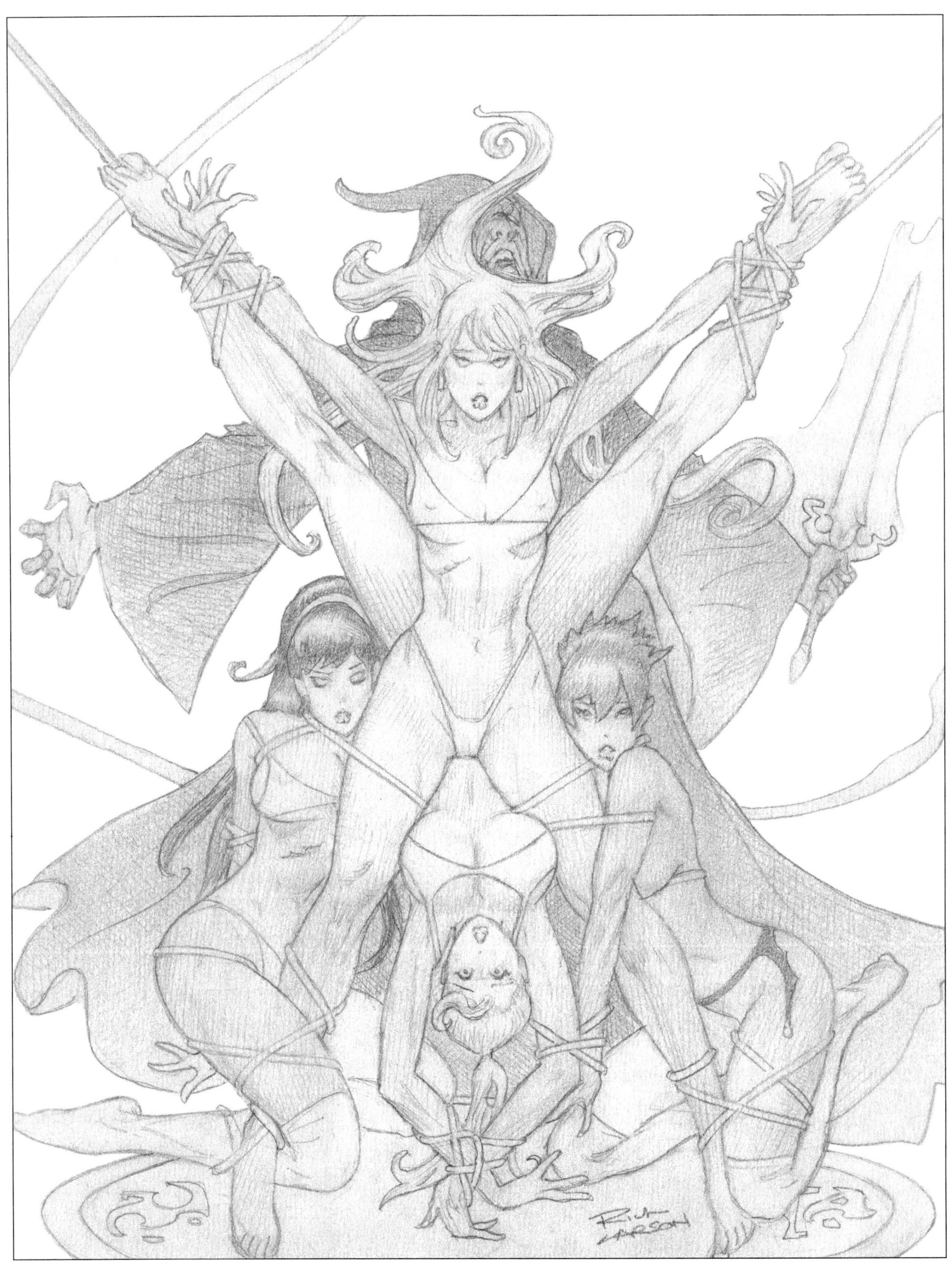

Accept This Sacrifice

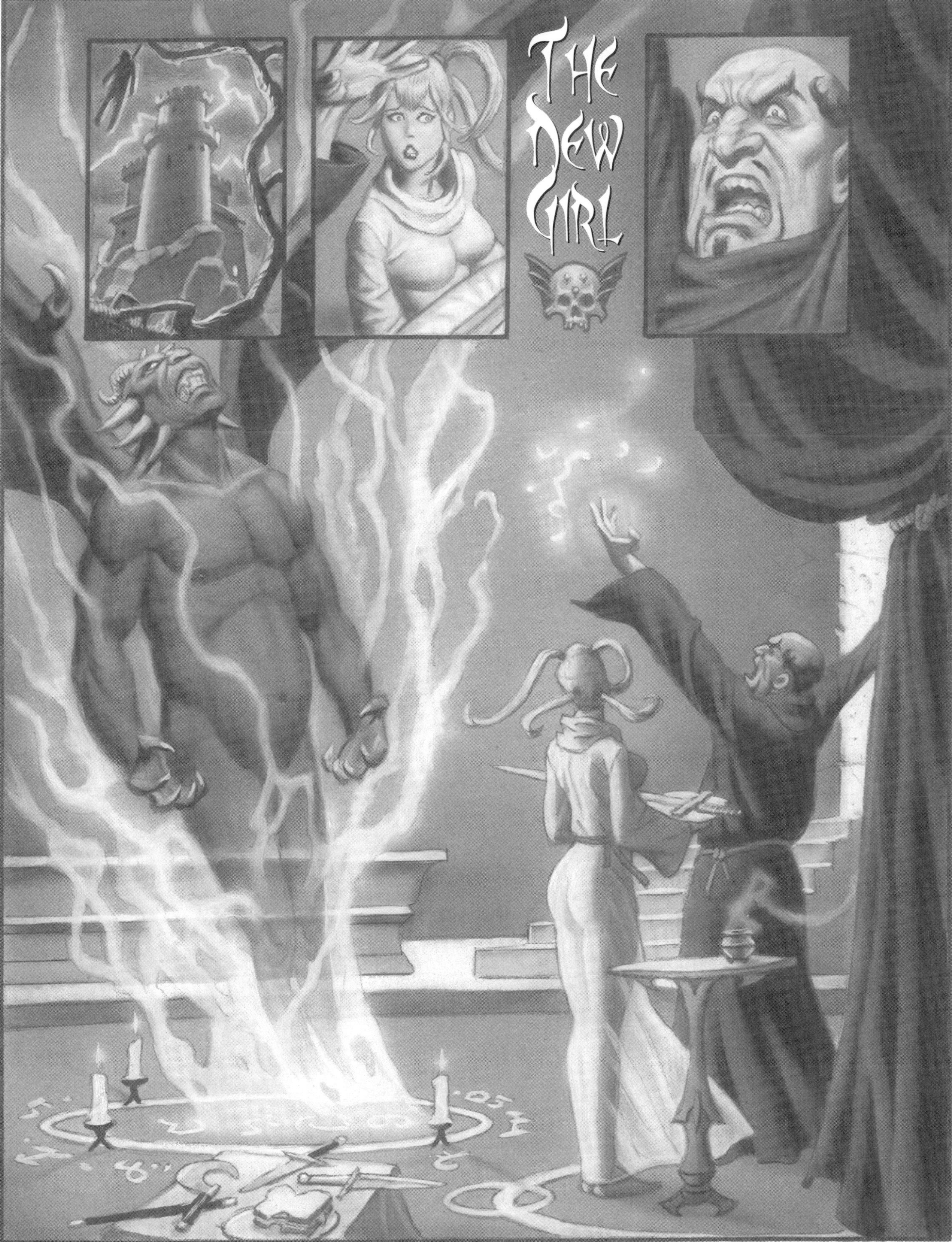
The New Girl

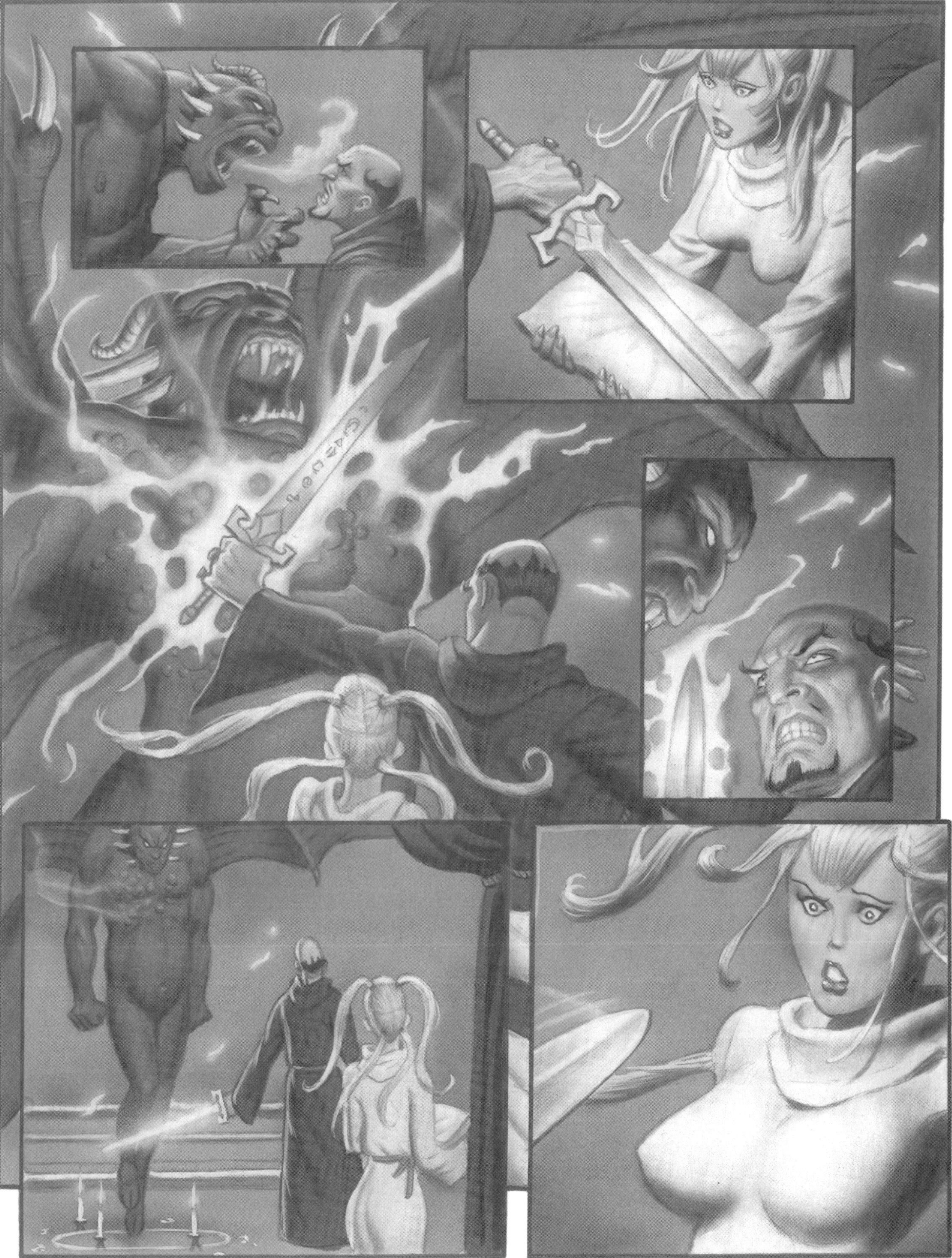

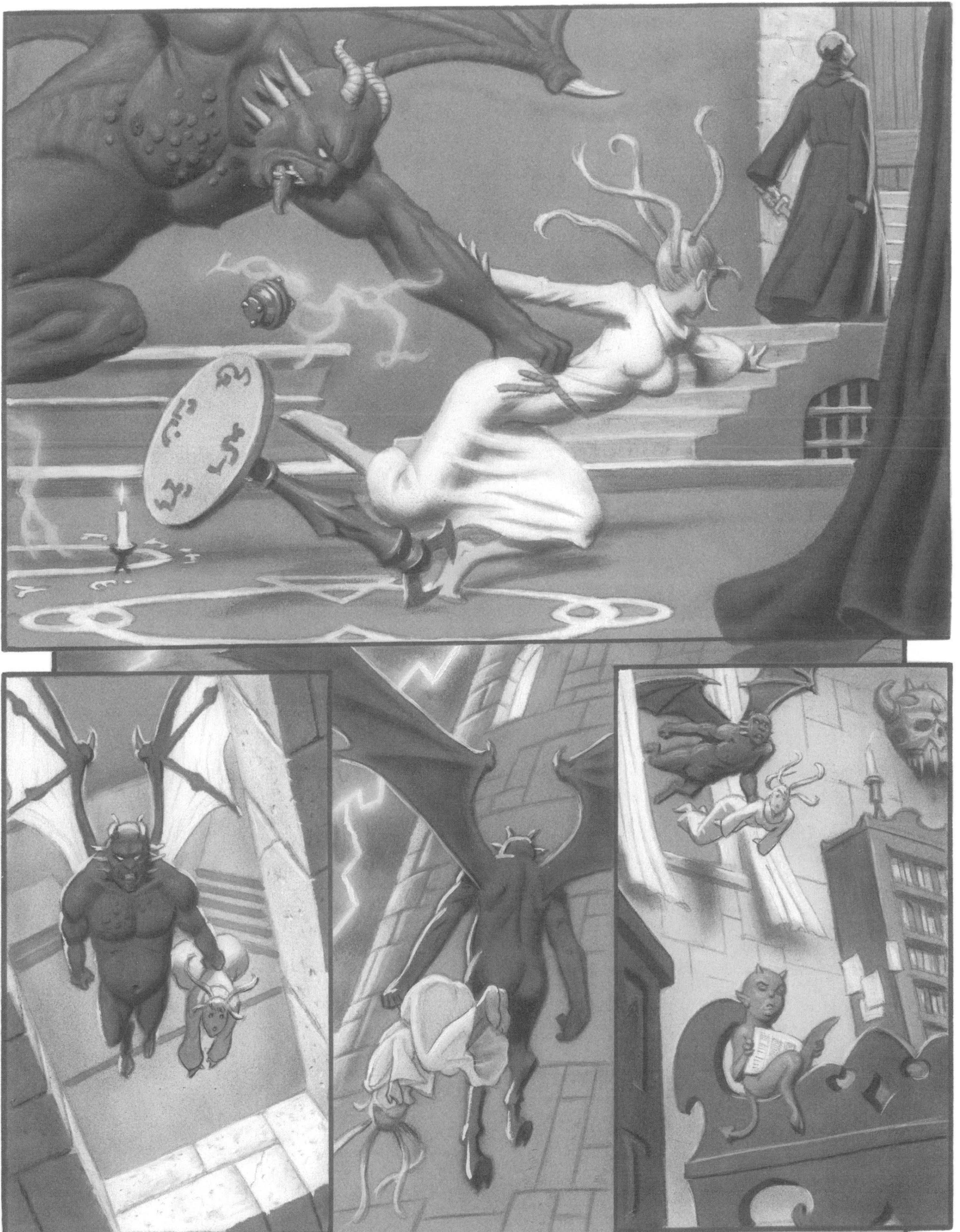

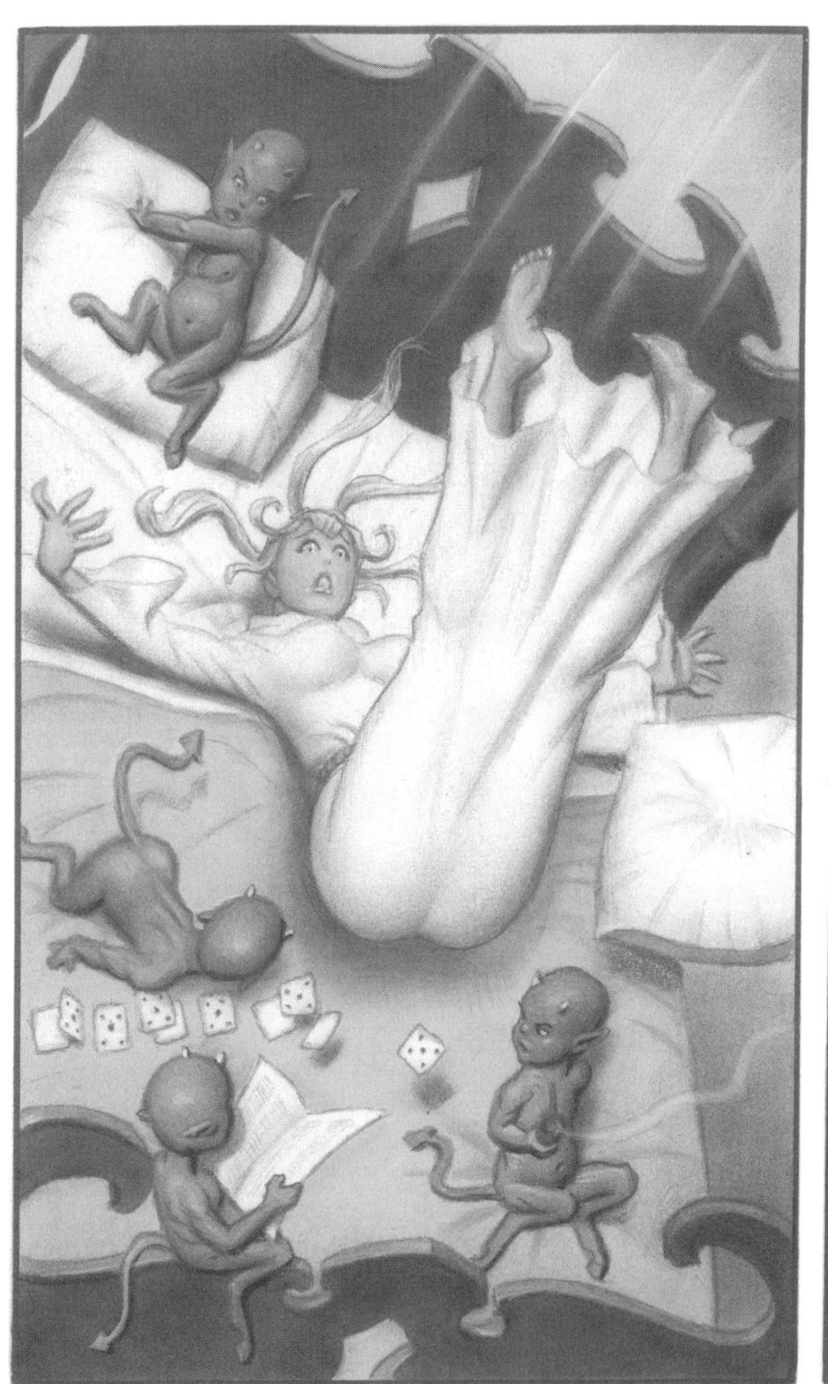

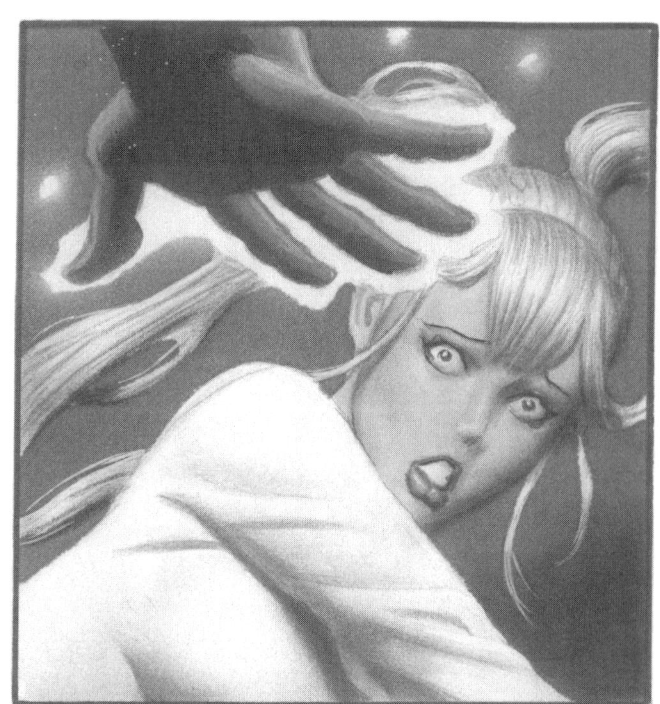

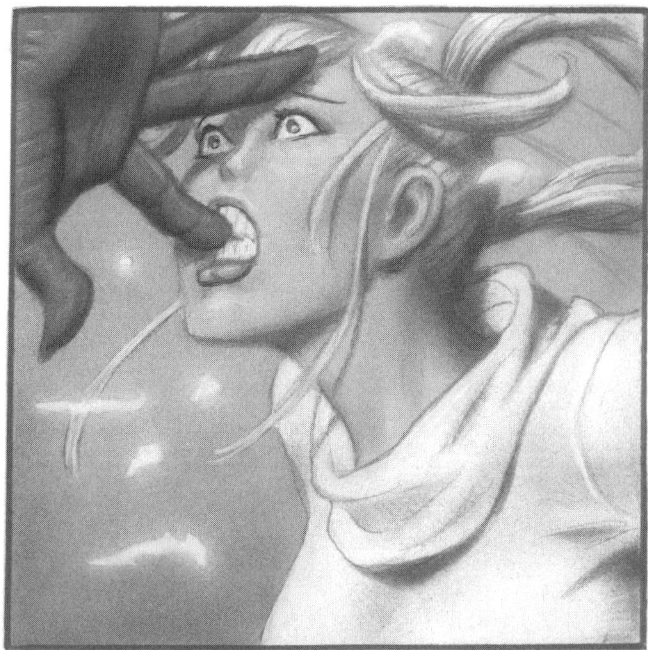

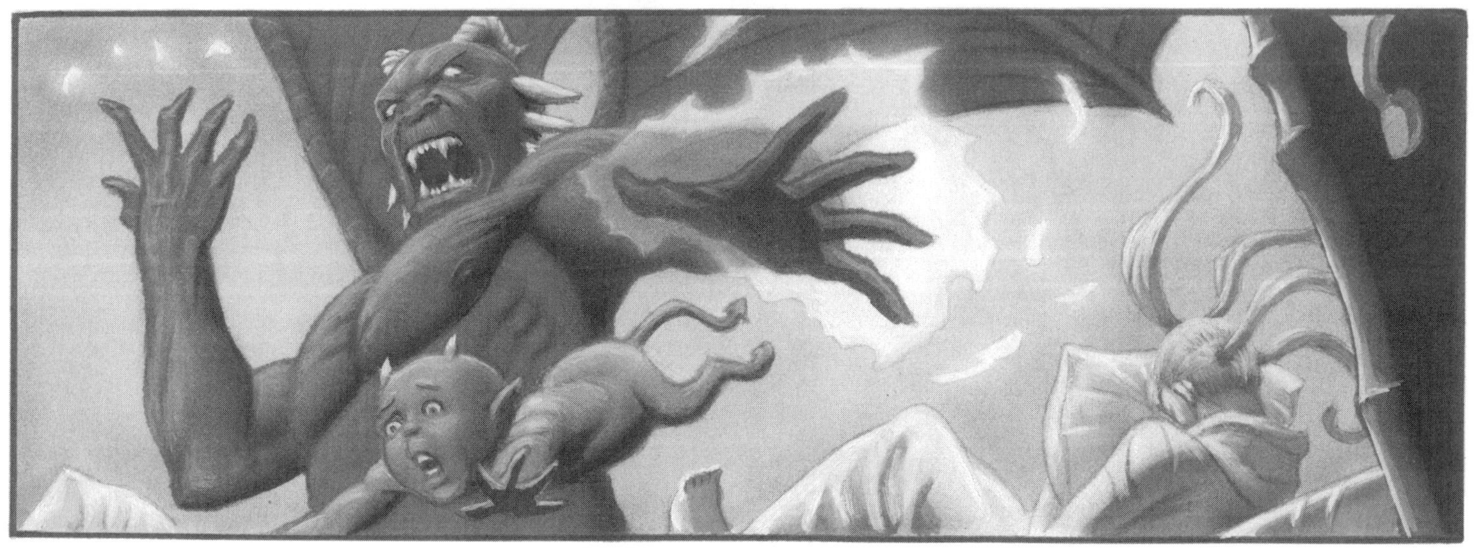

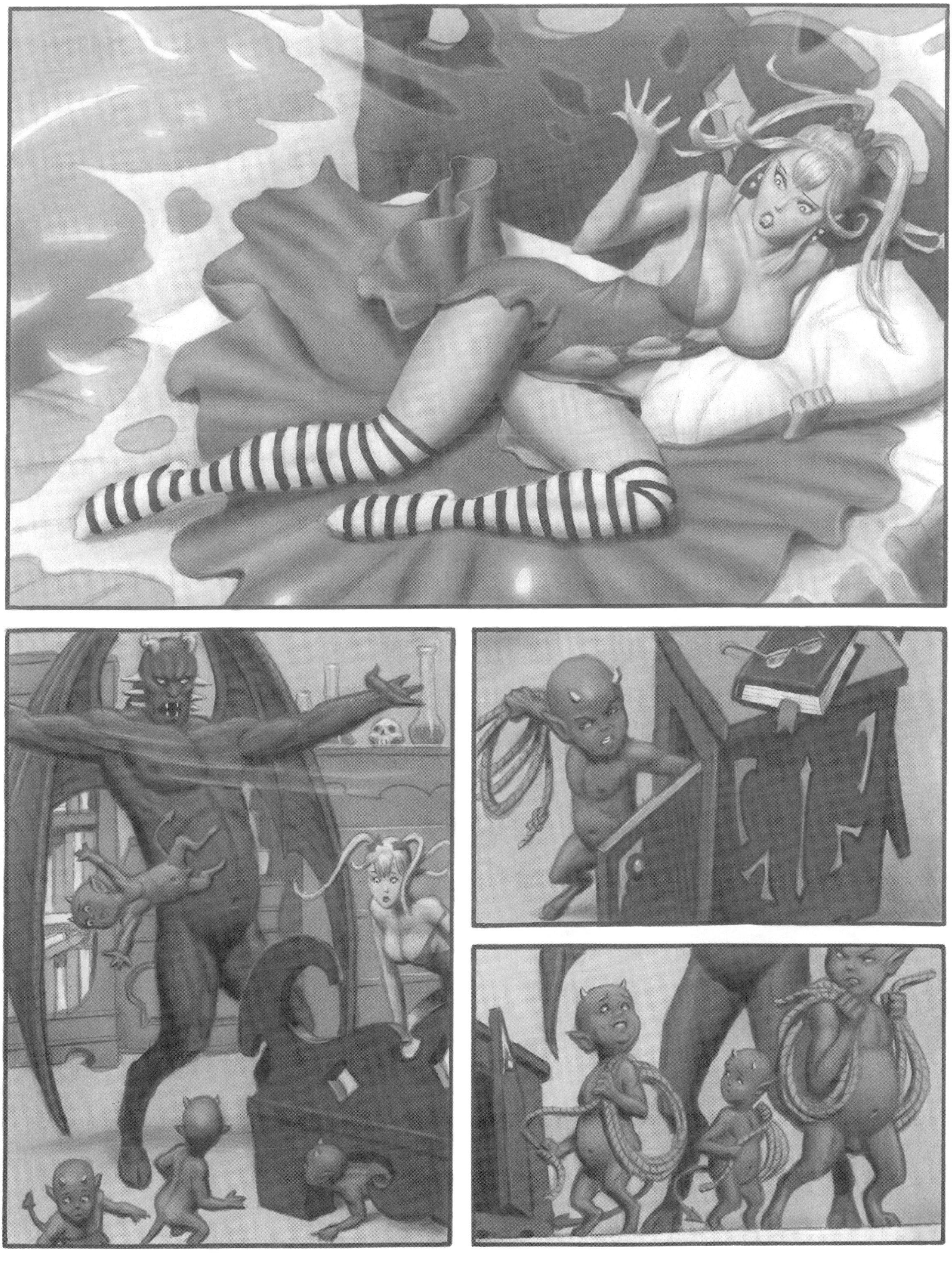

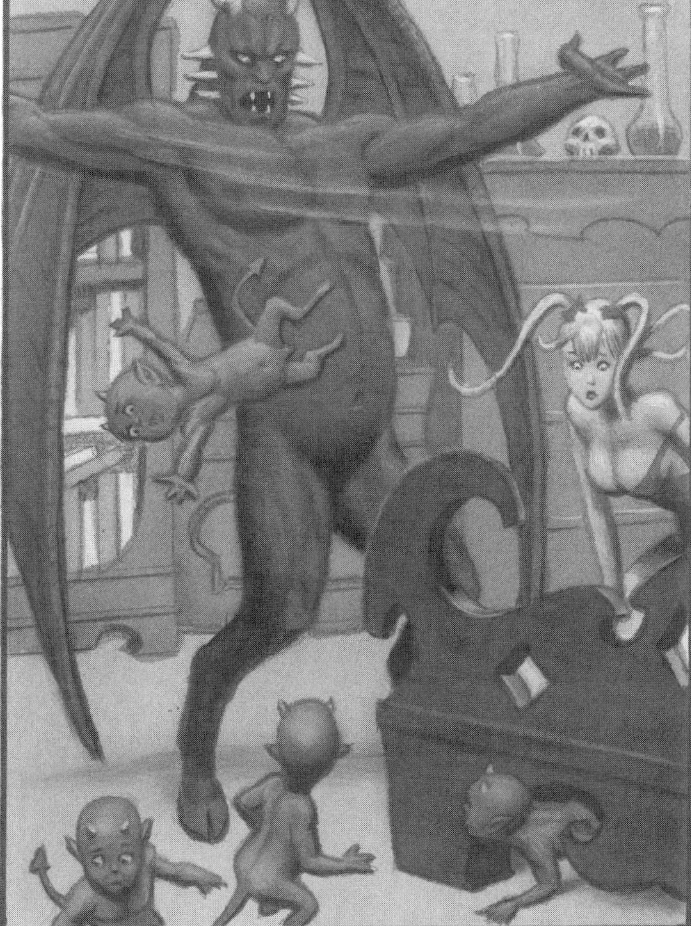
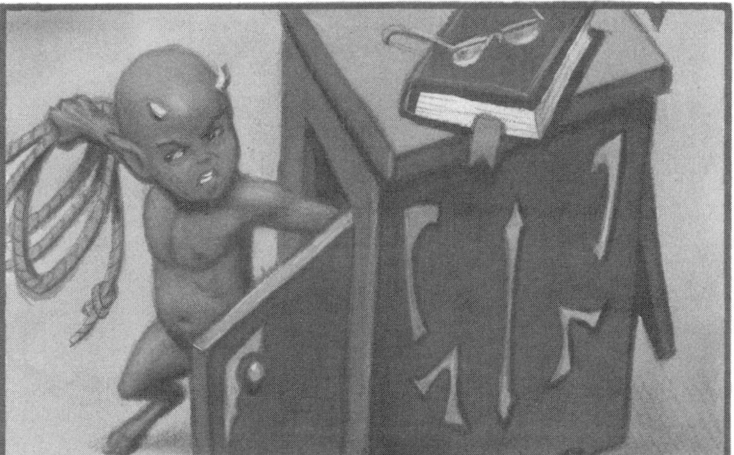
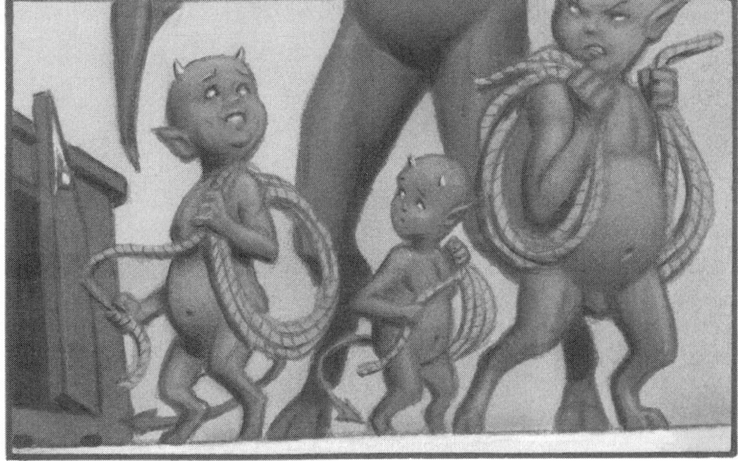

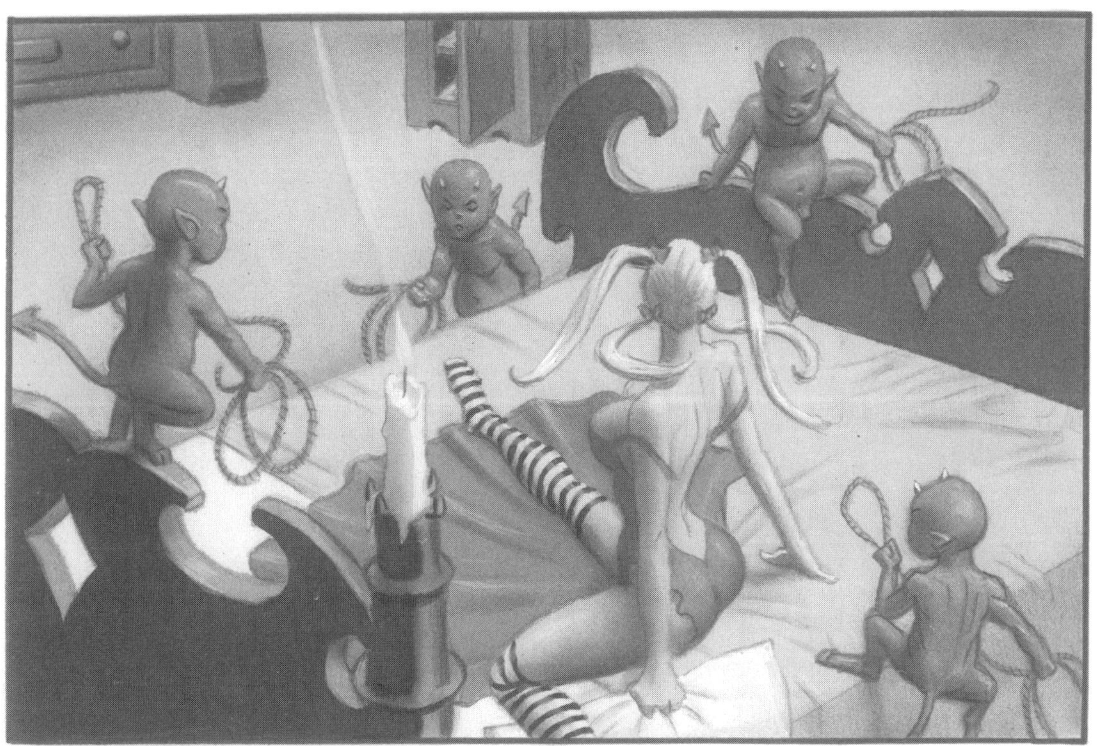
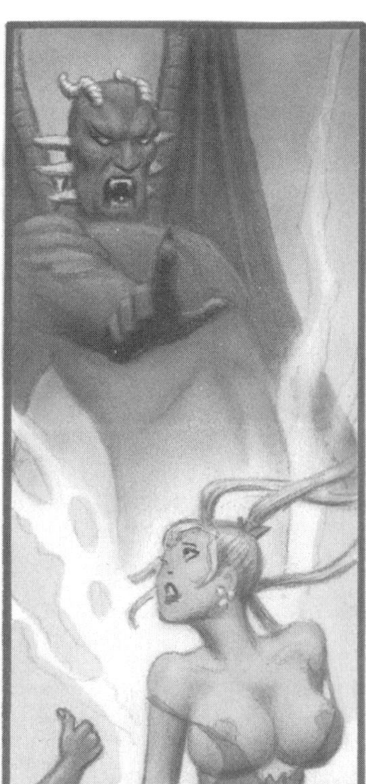
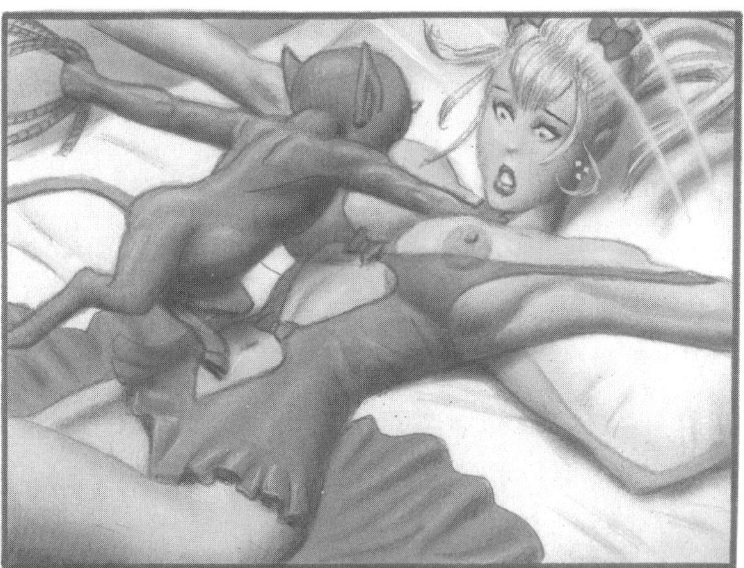
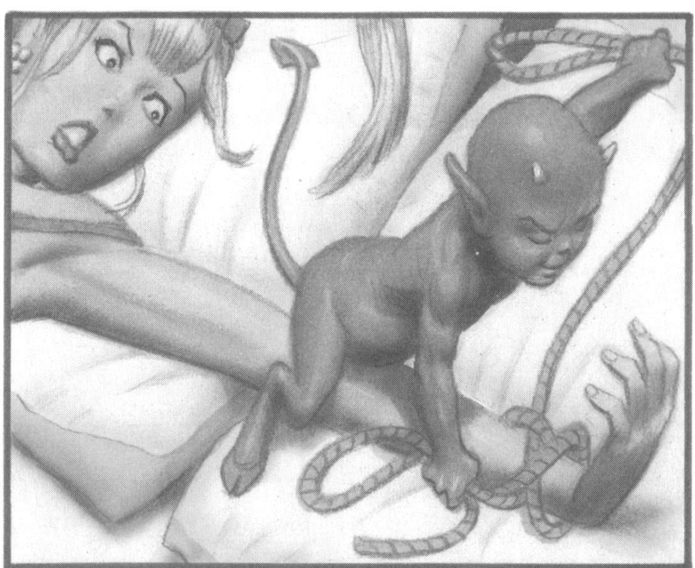
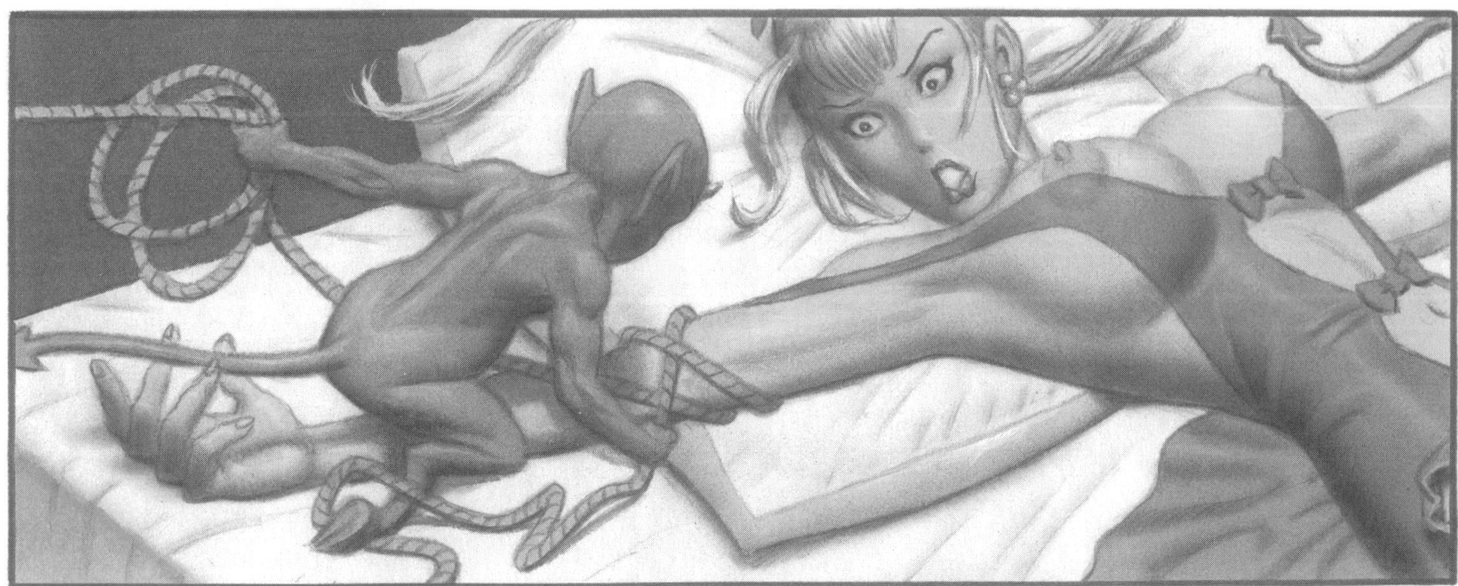

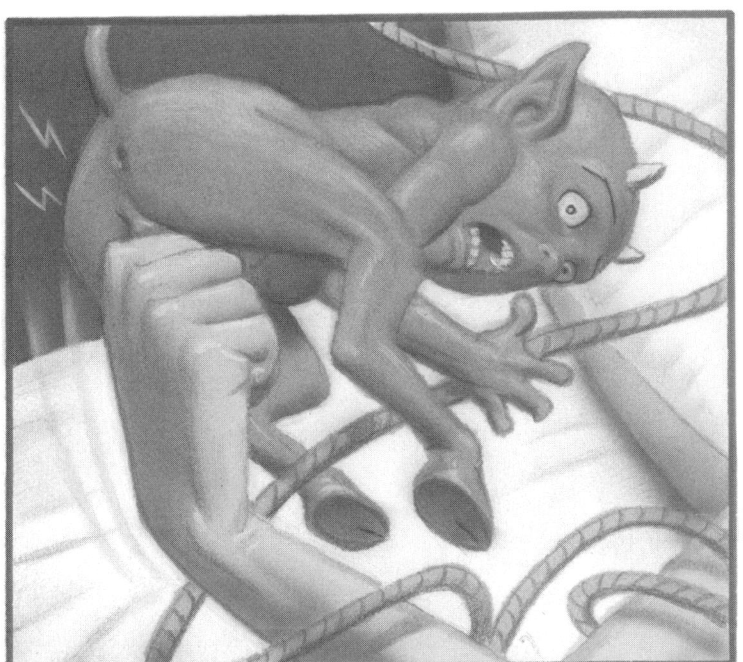
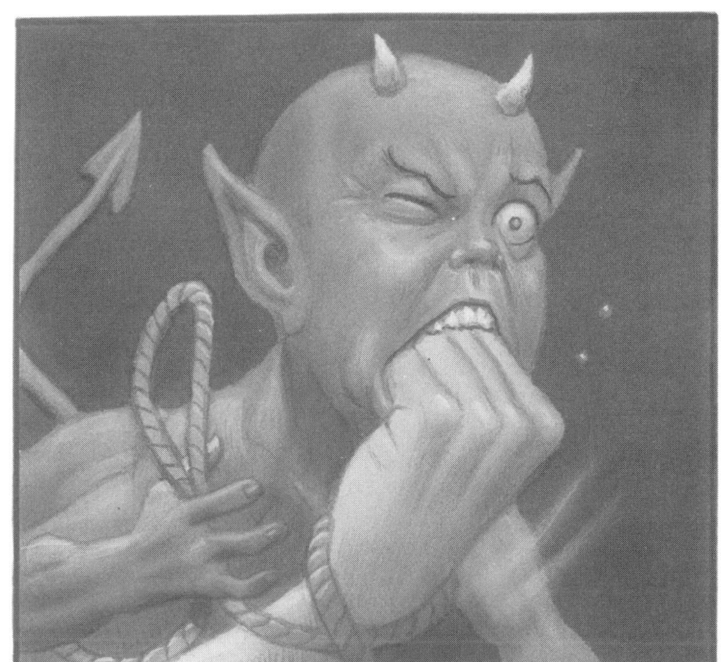
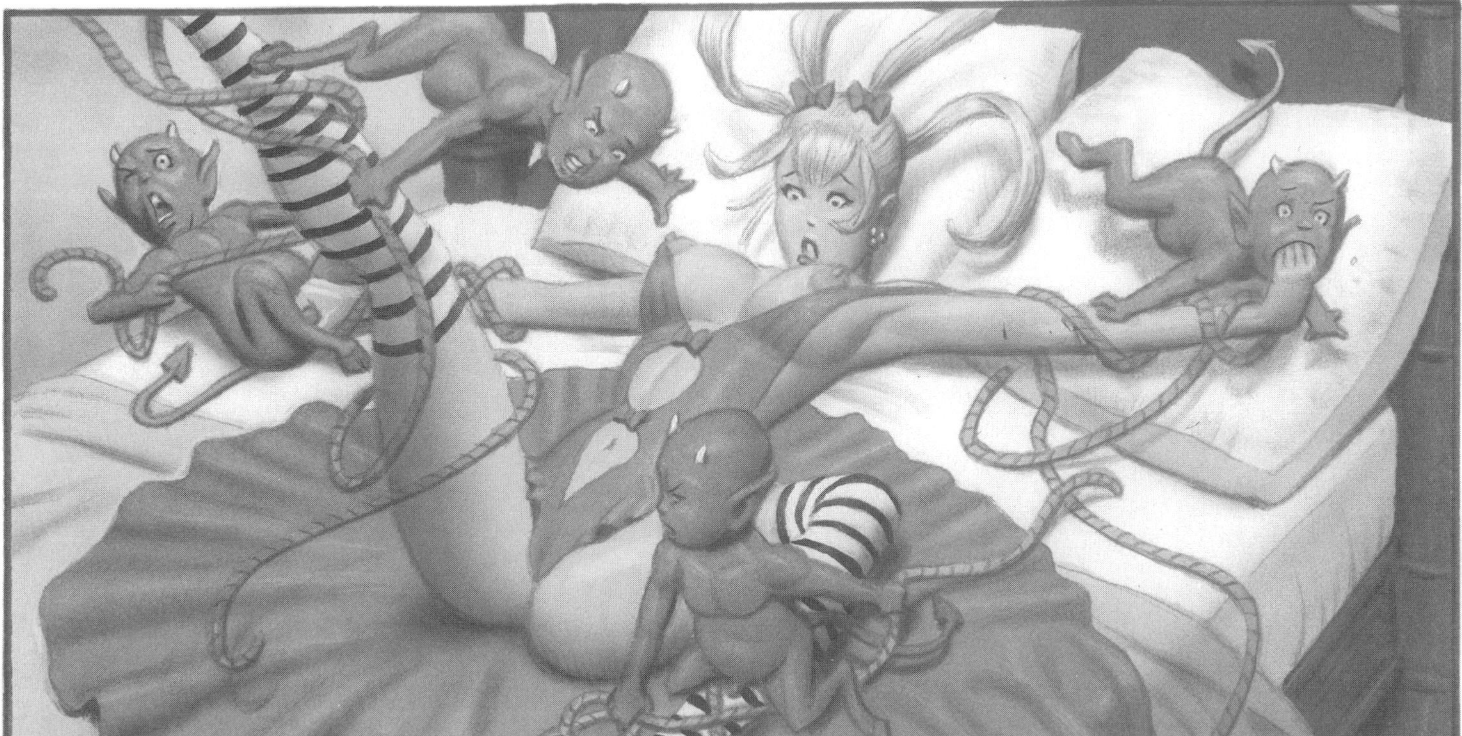
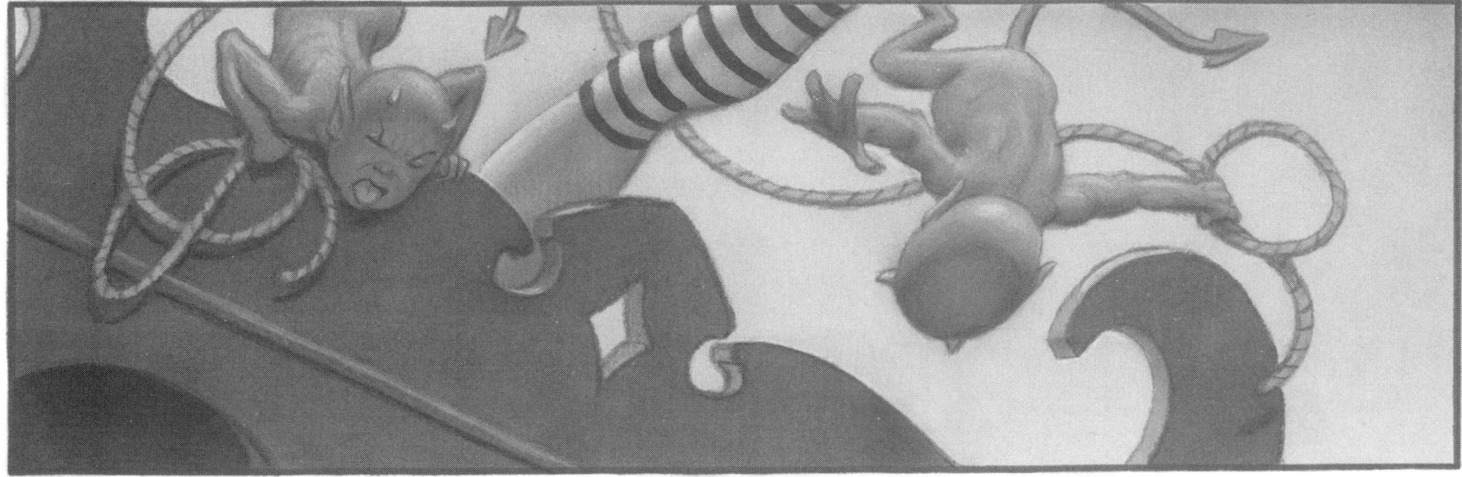

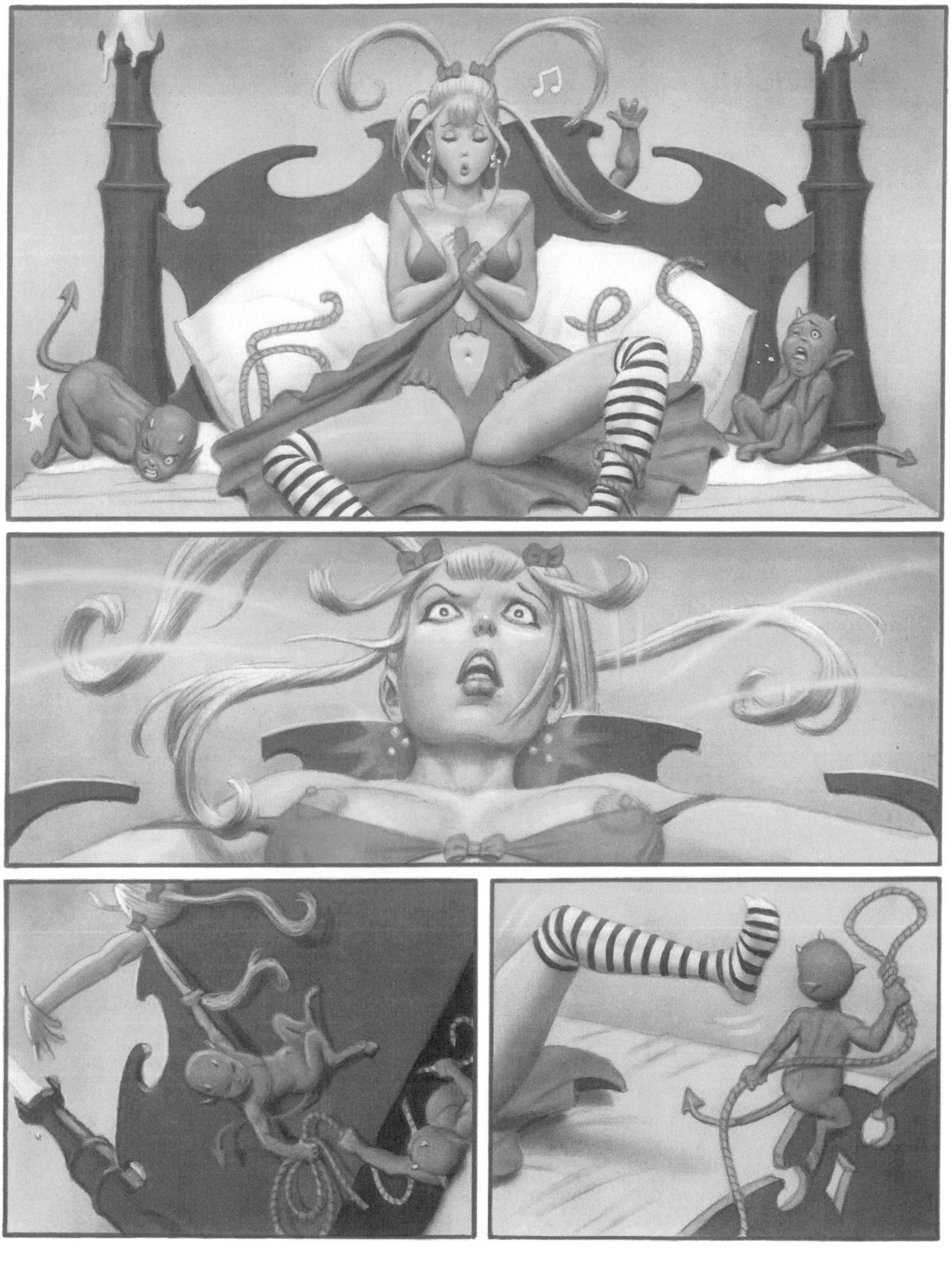

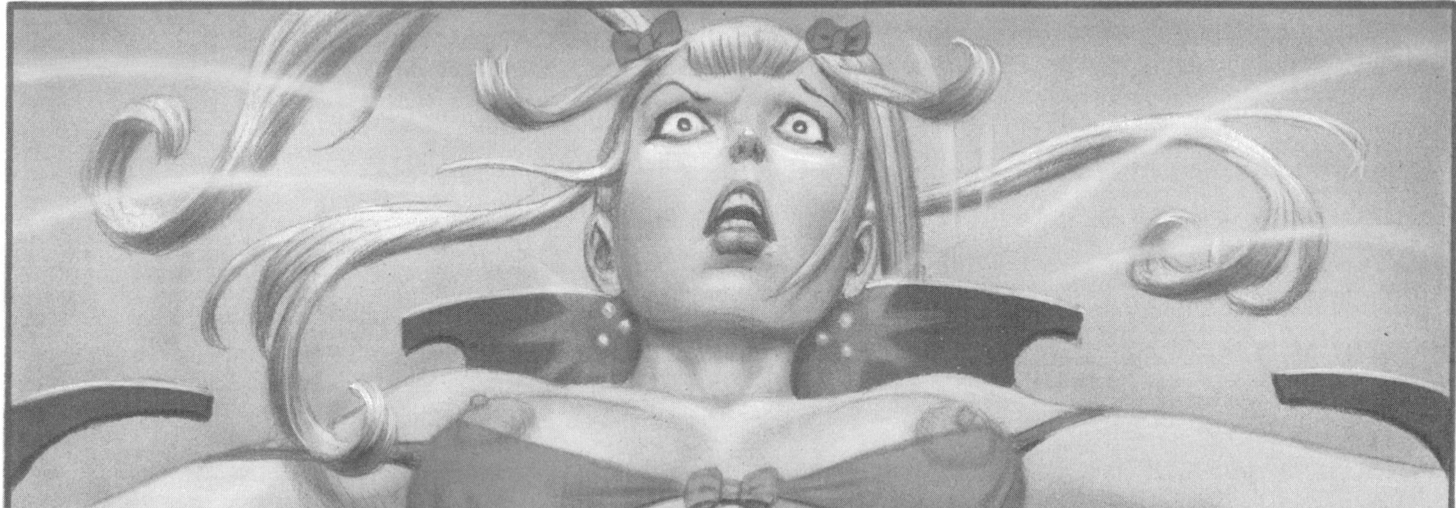

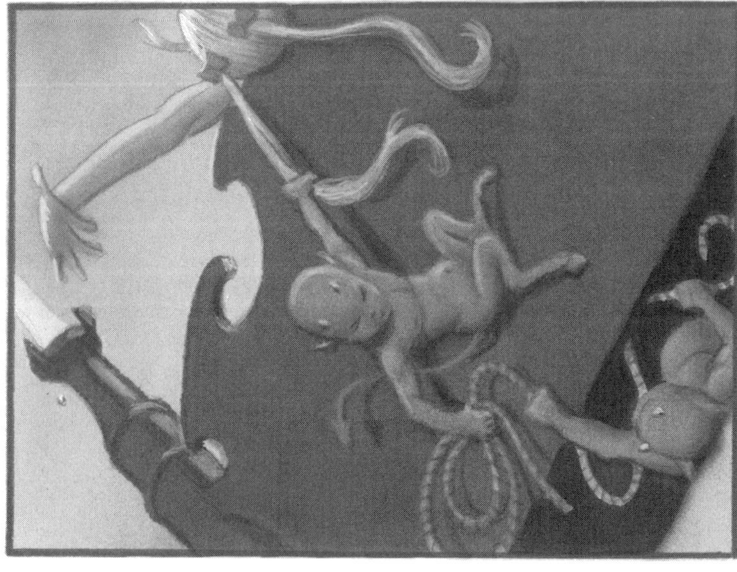

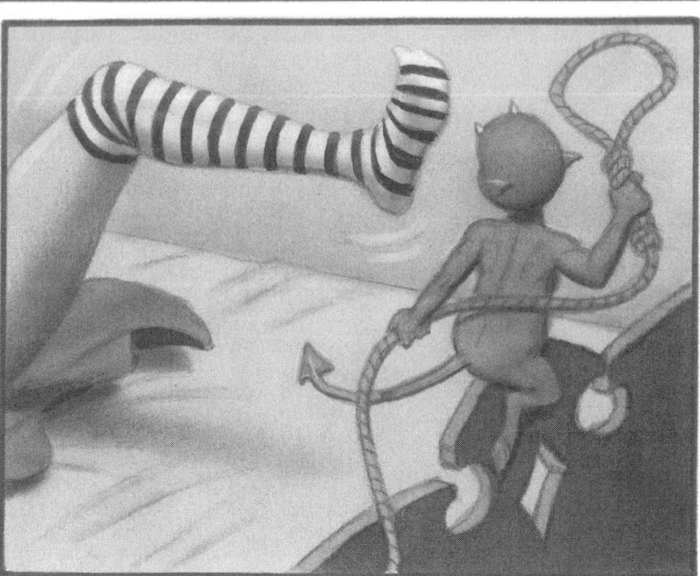

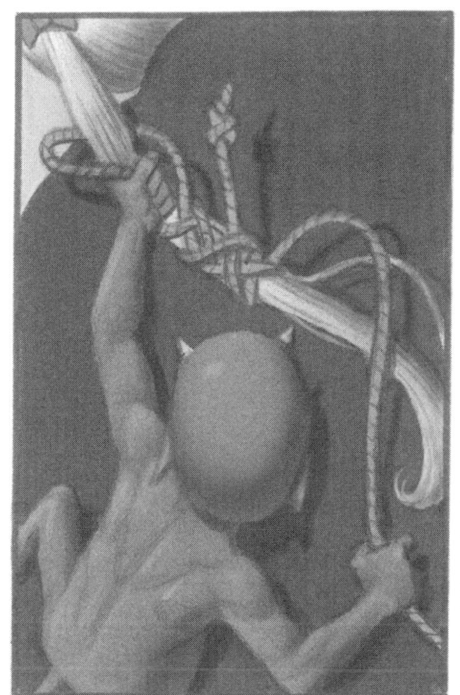
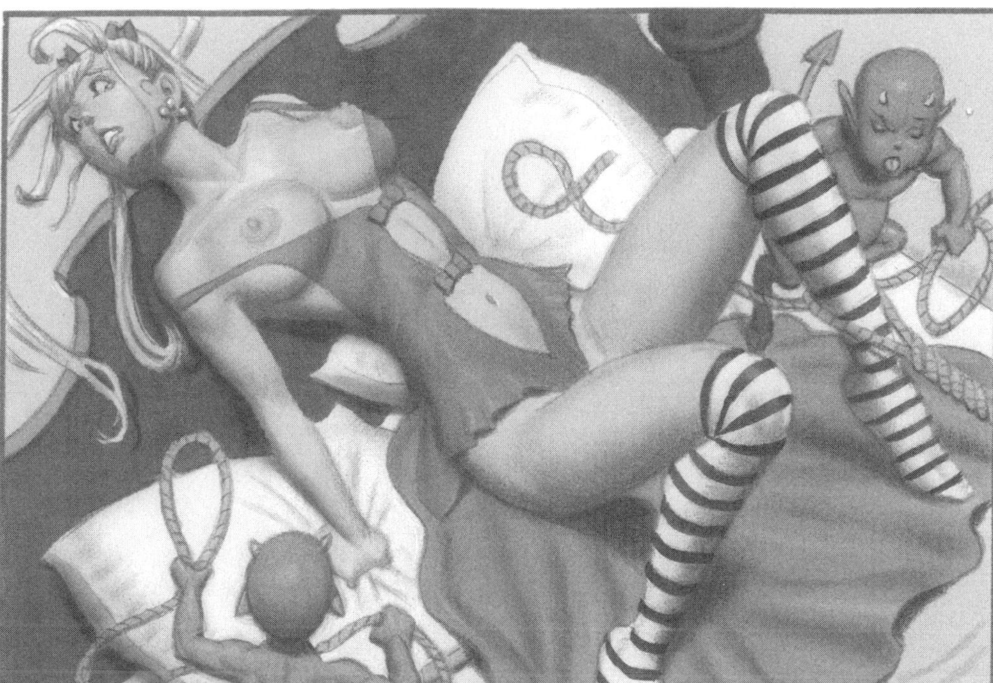
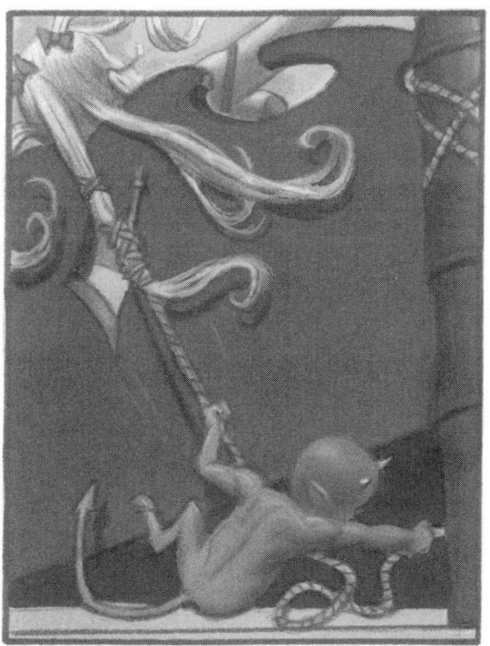
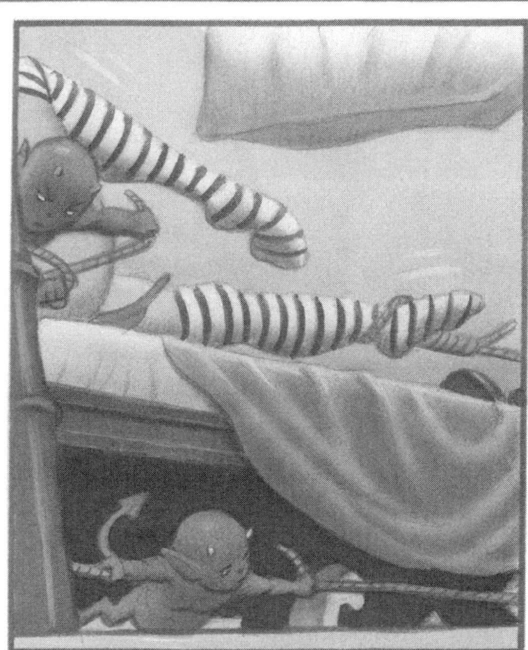
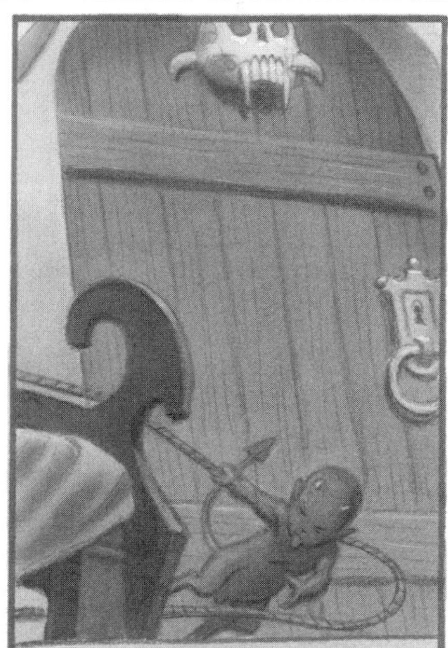
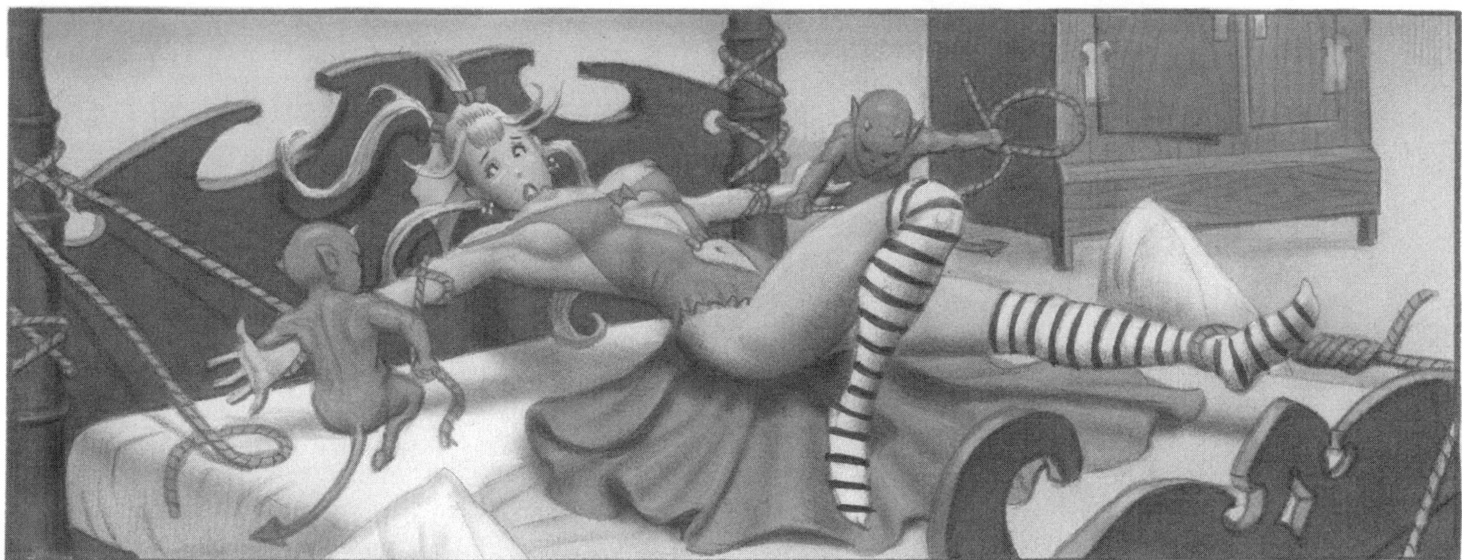

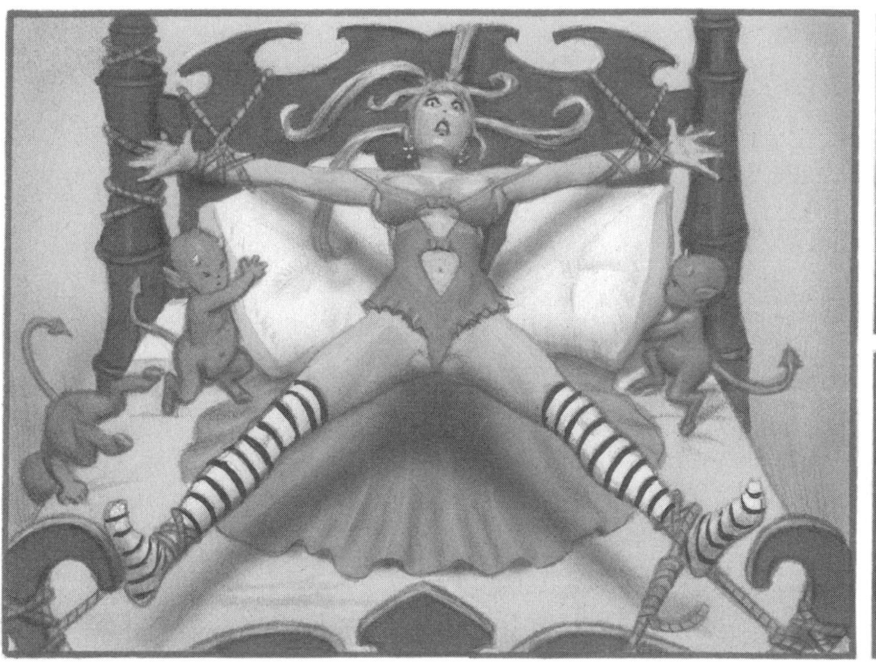
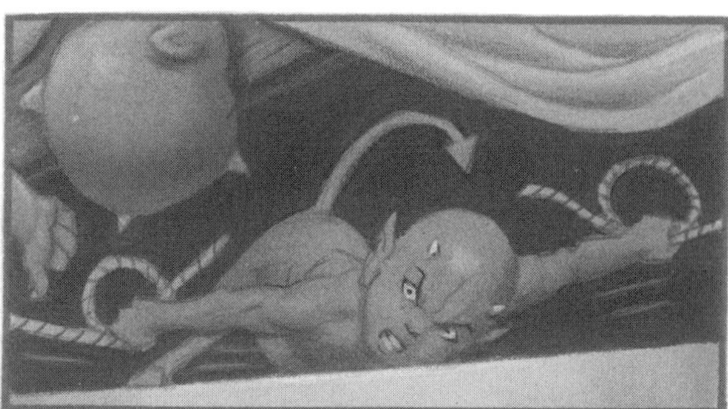
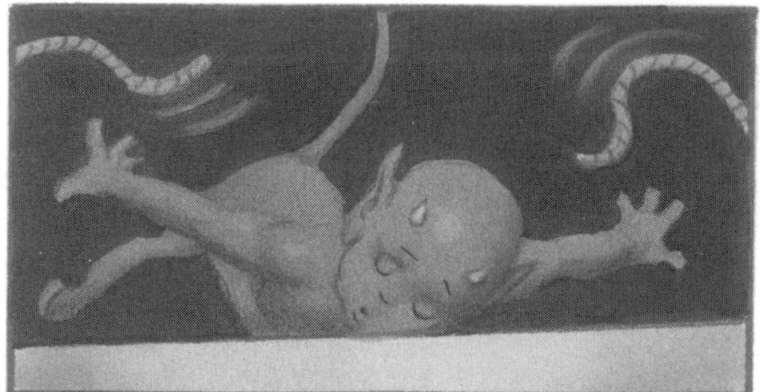
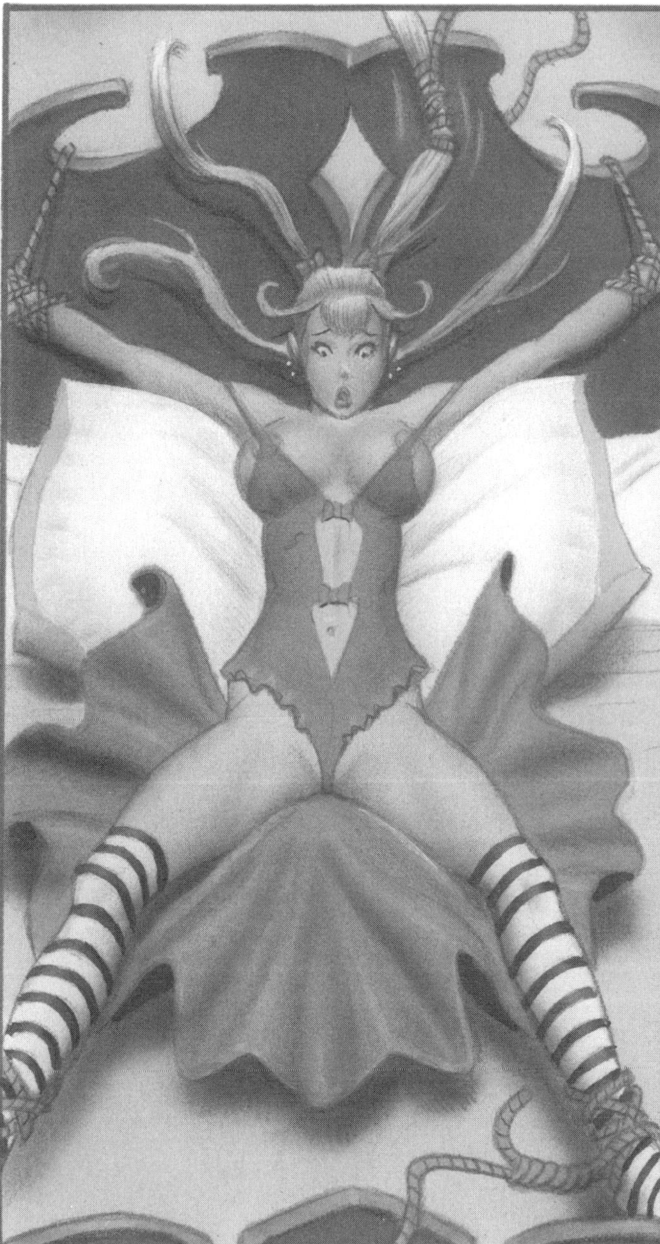
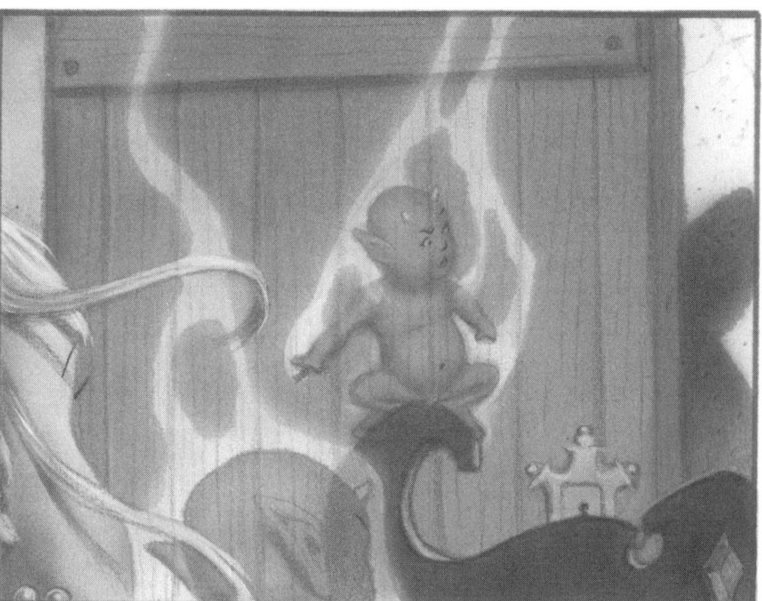
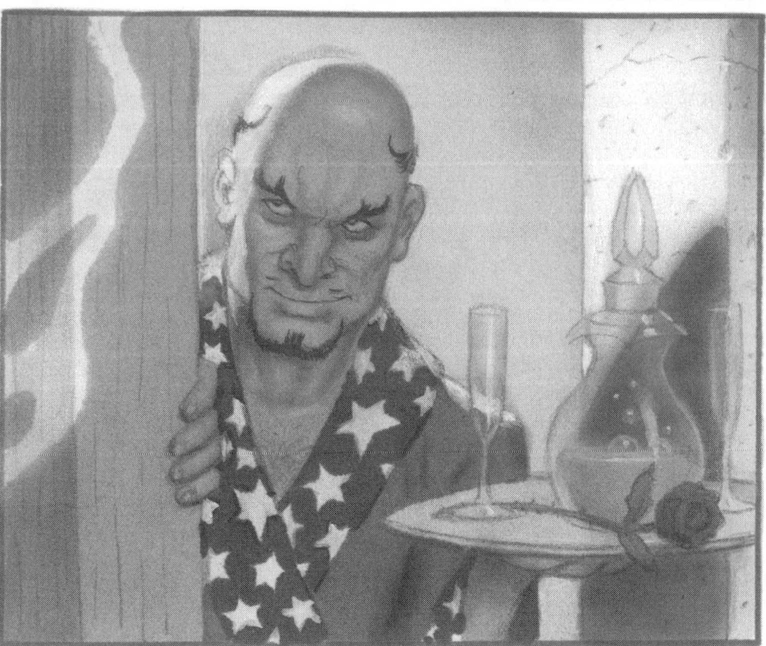

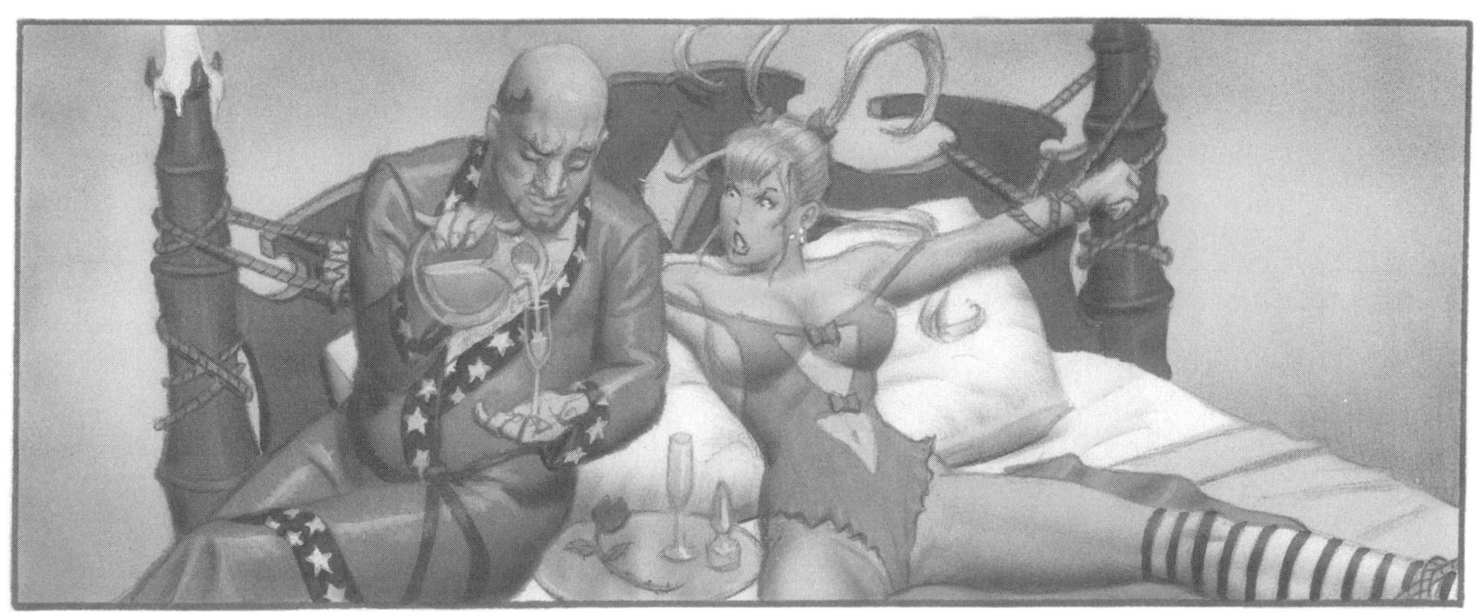
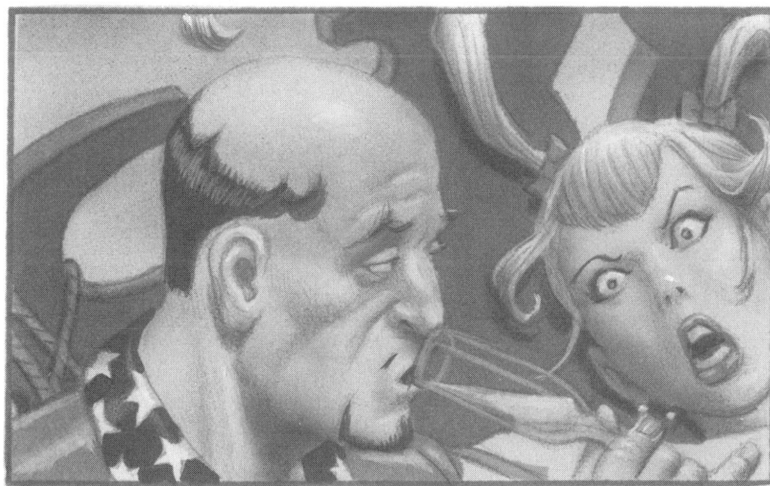
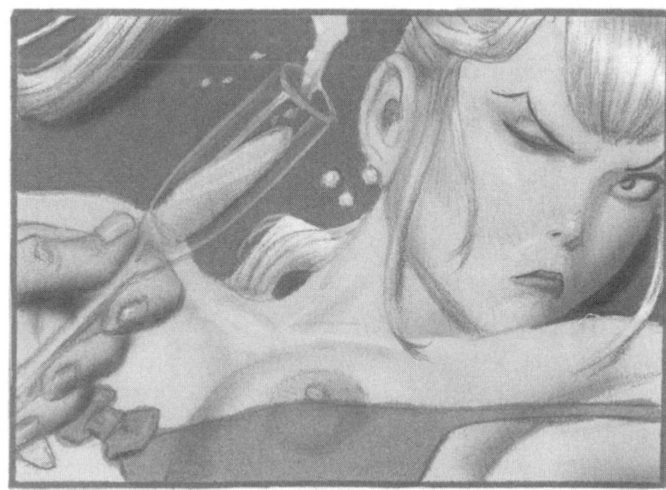
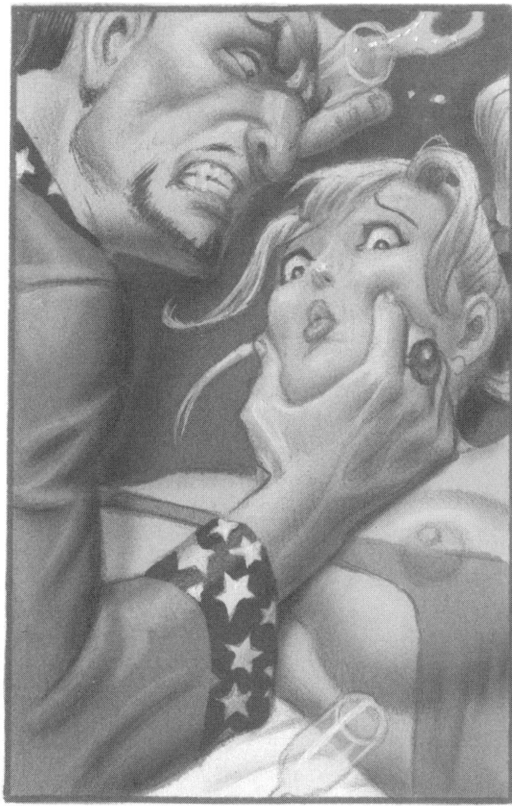
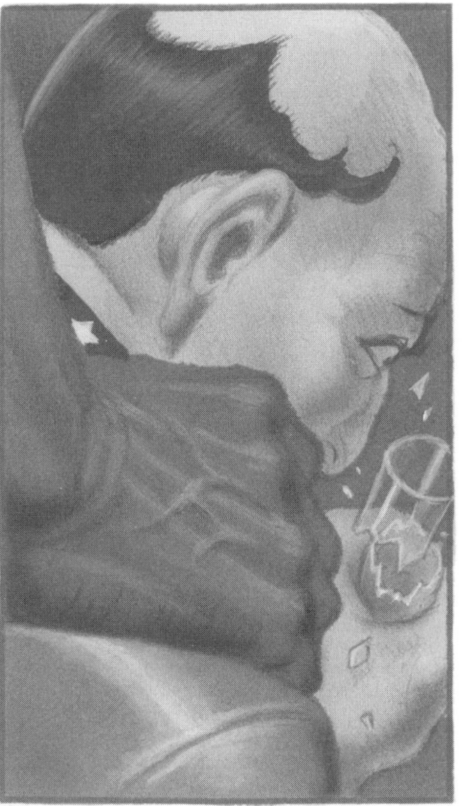
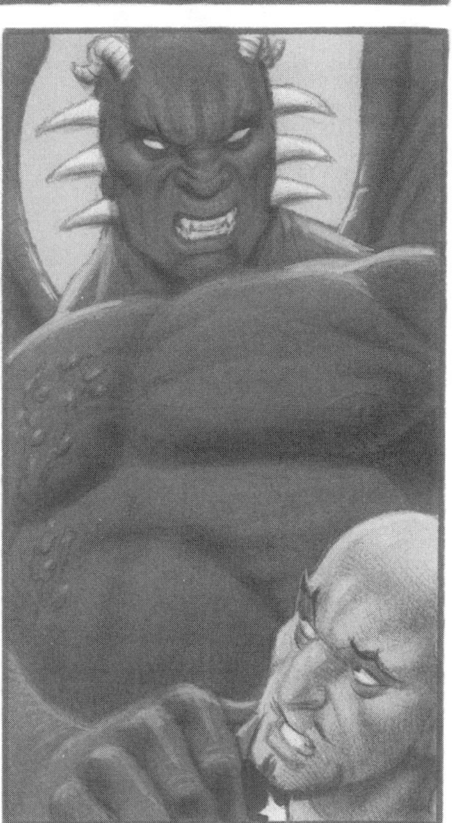

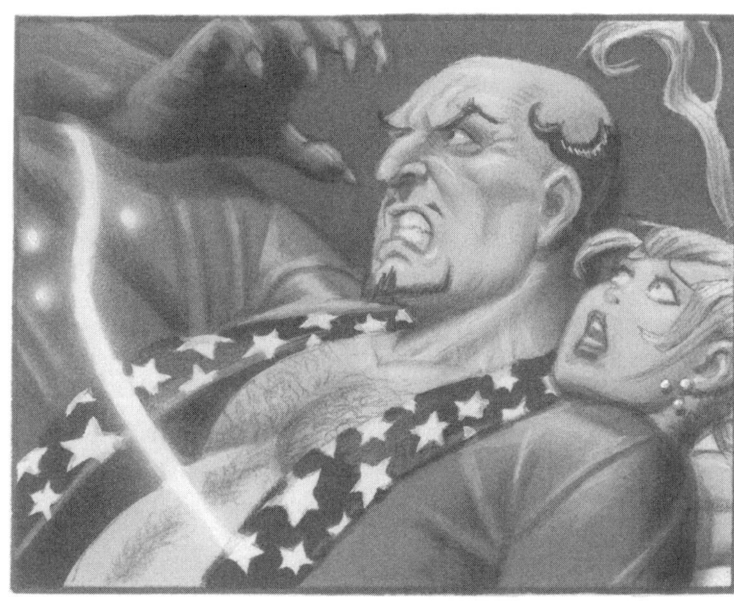

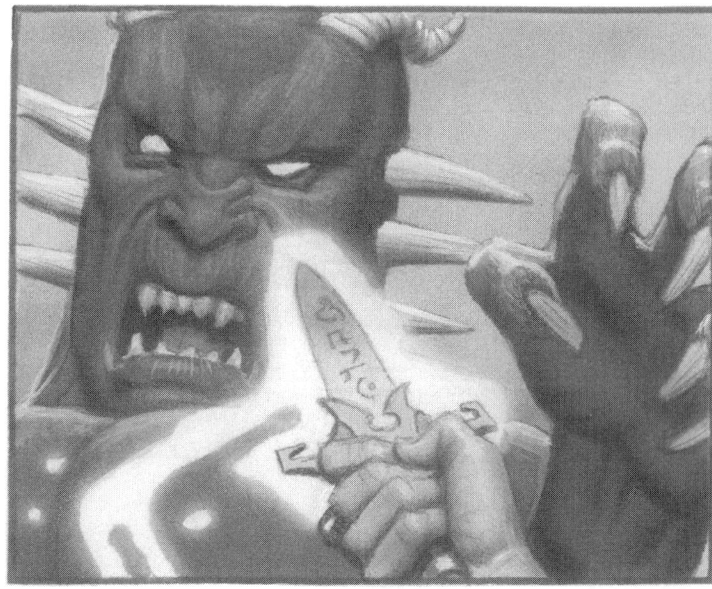

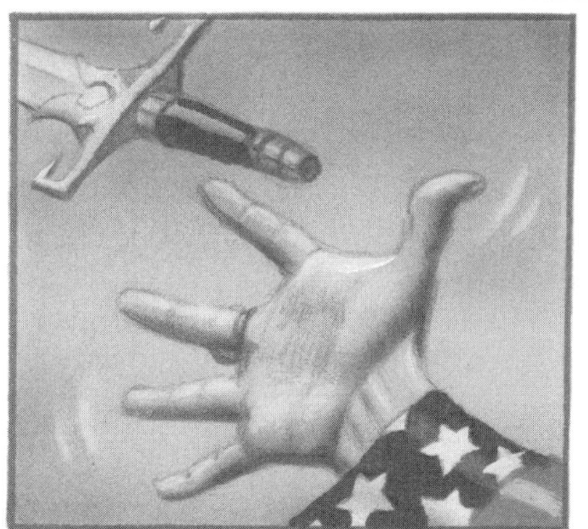

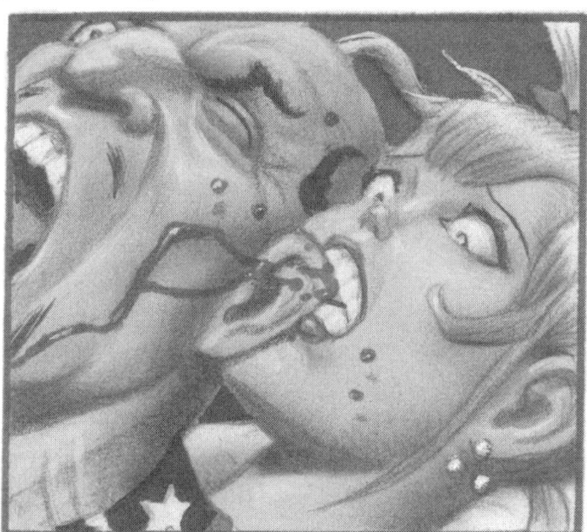

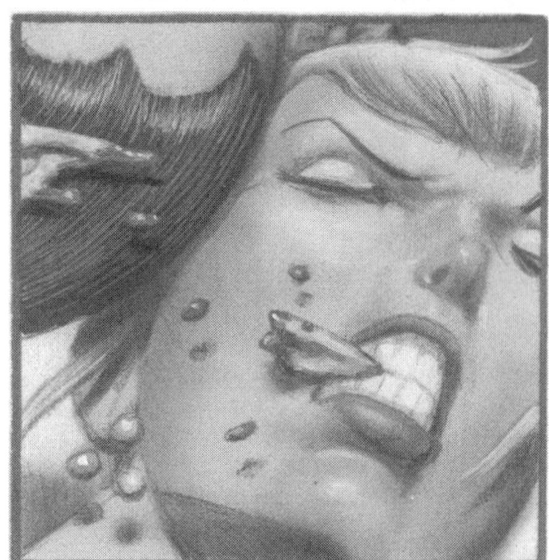

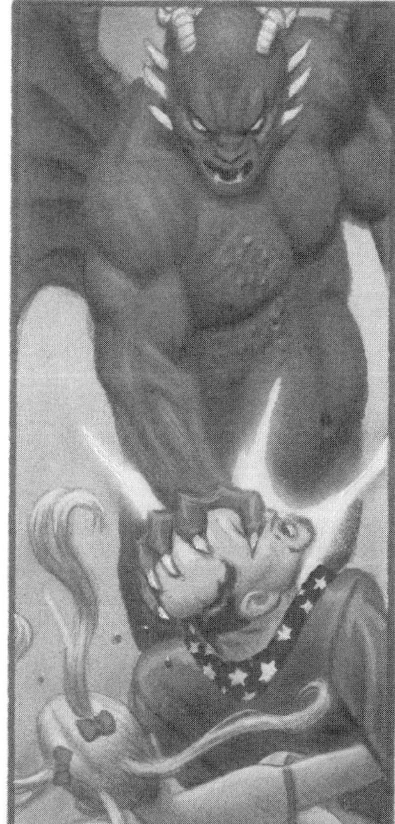

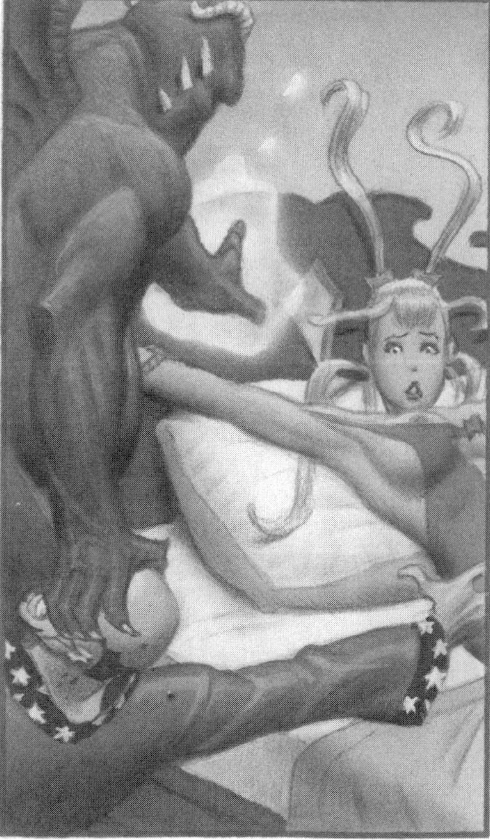

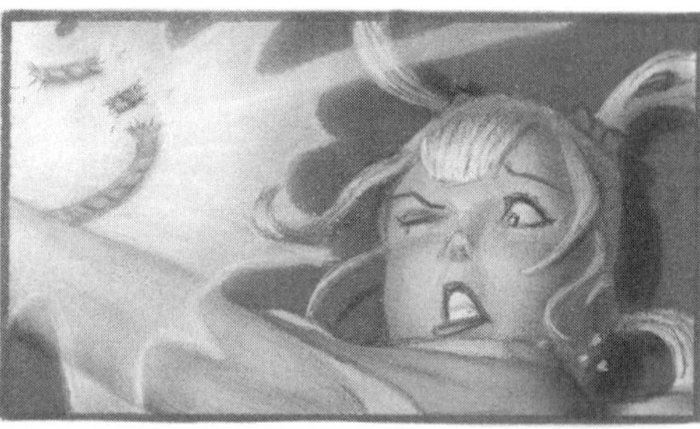

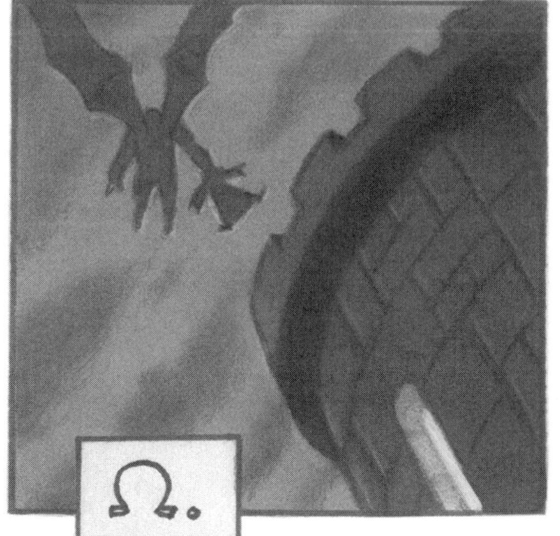

Ω.

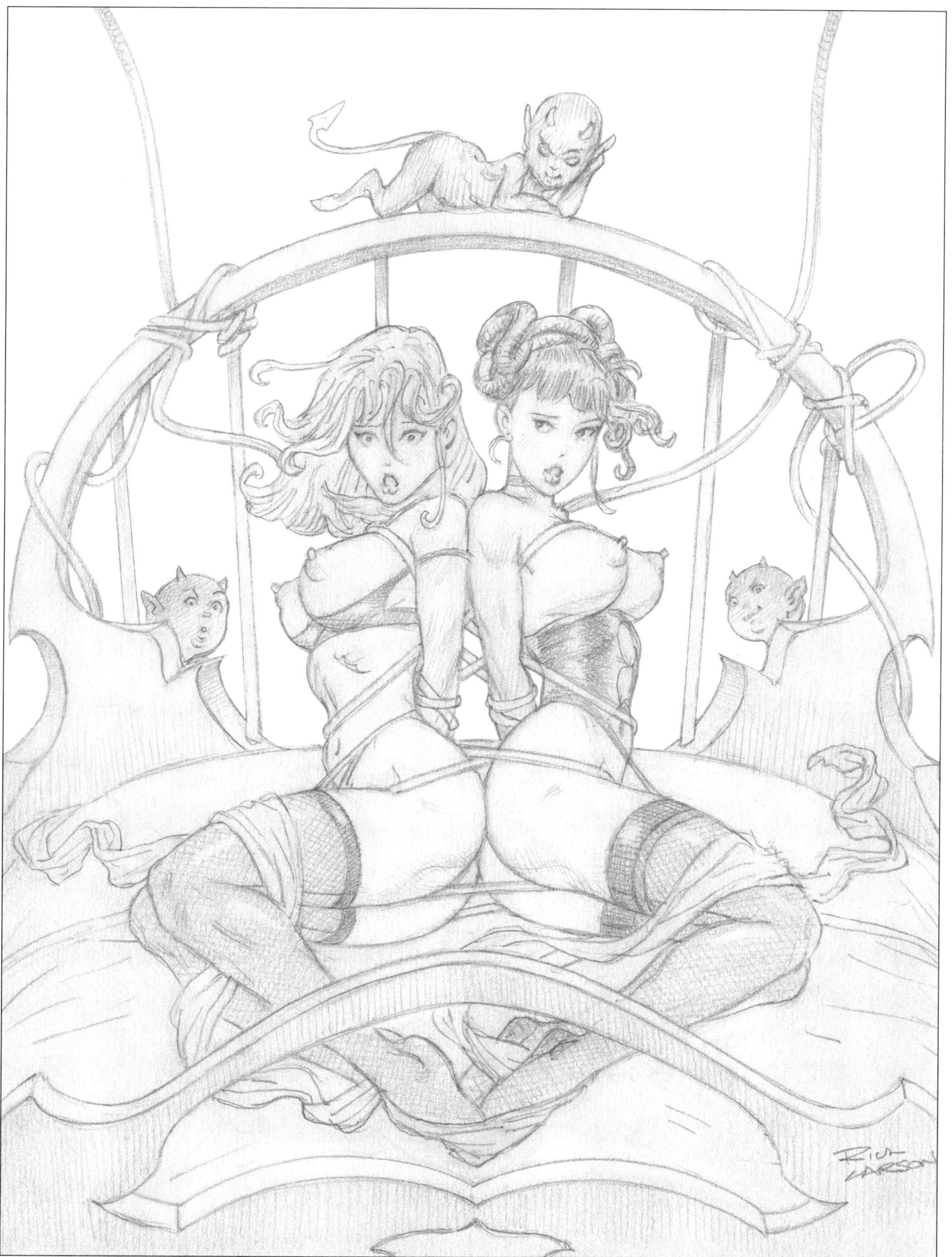

Bedtime Companions

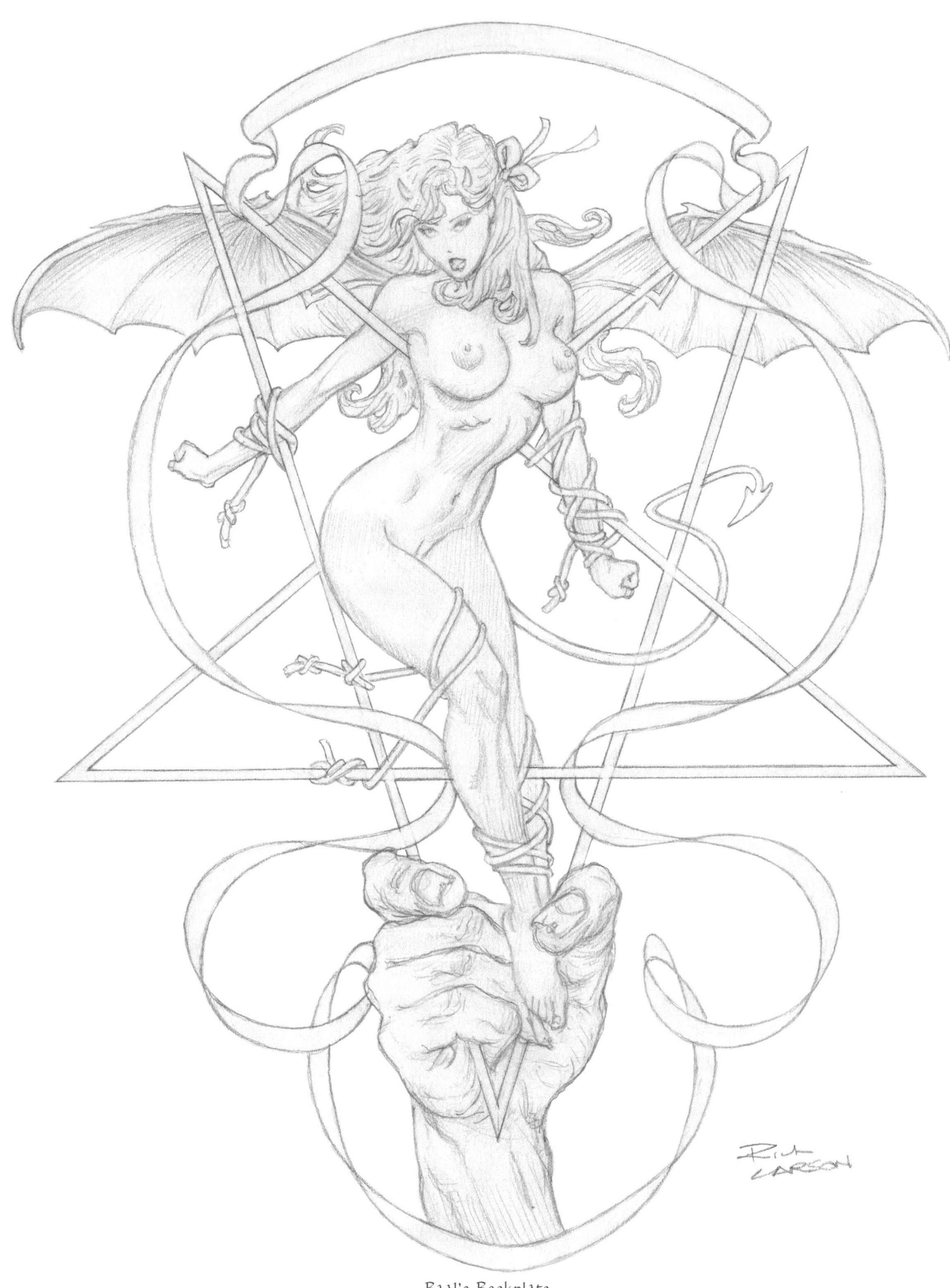

Baal's Bookplate

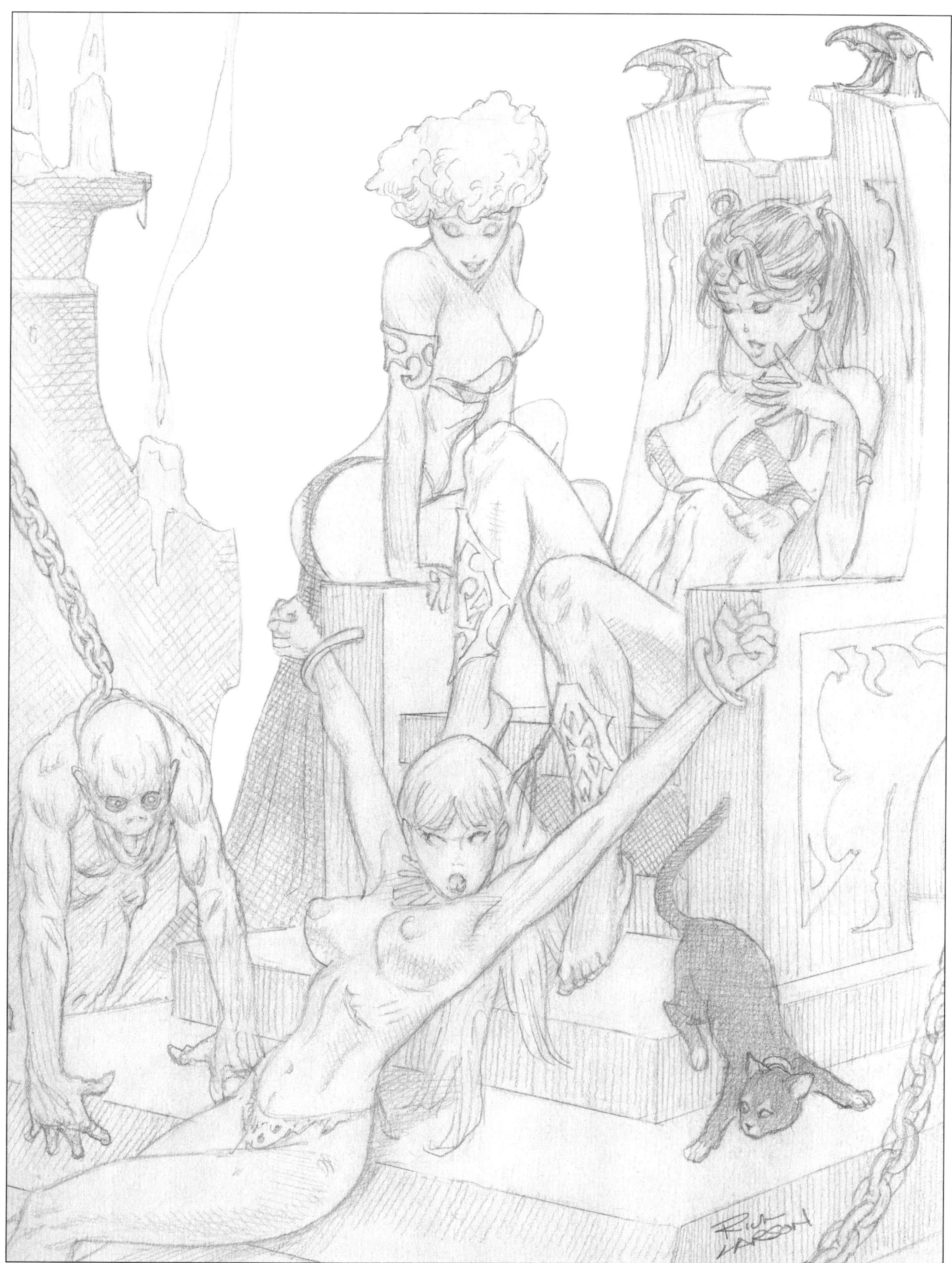

New Pet

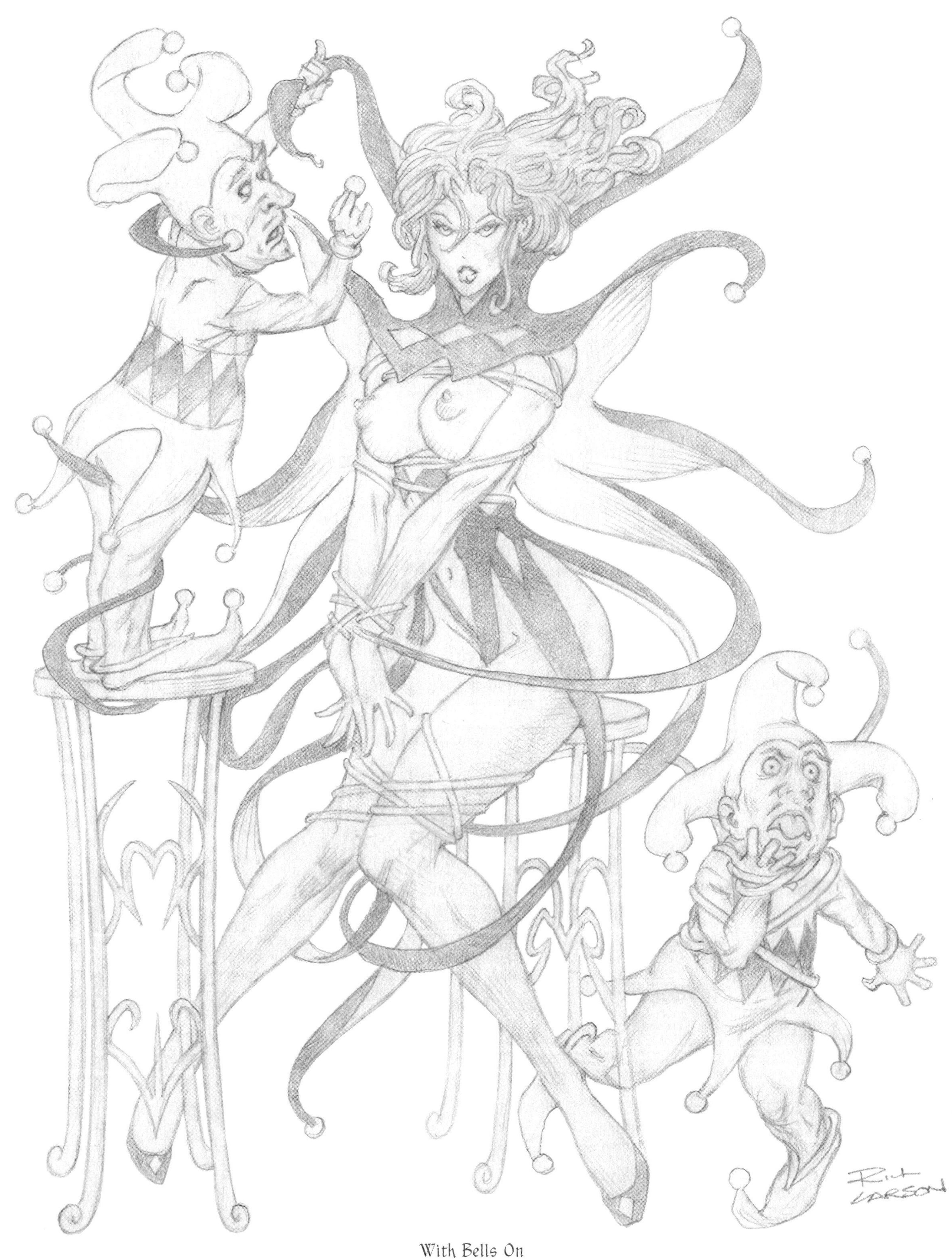

With Bells On

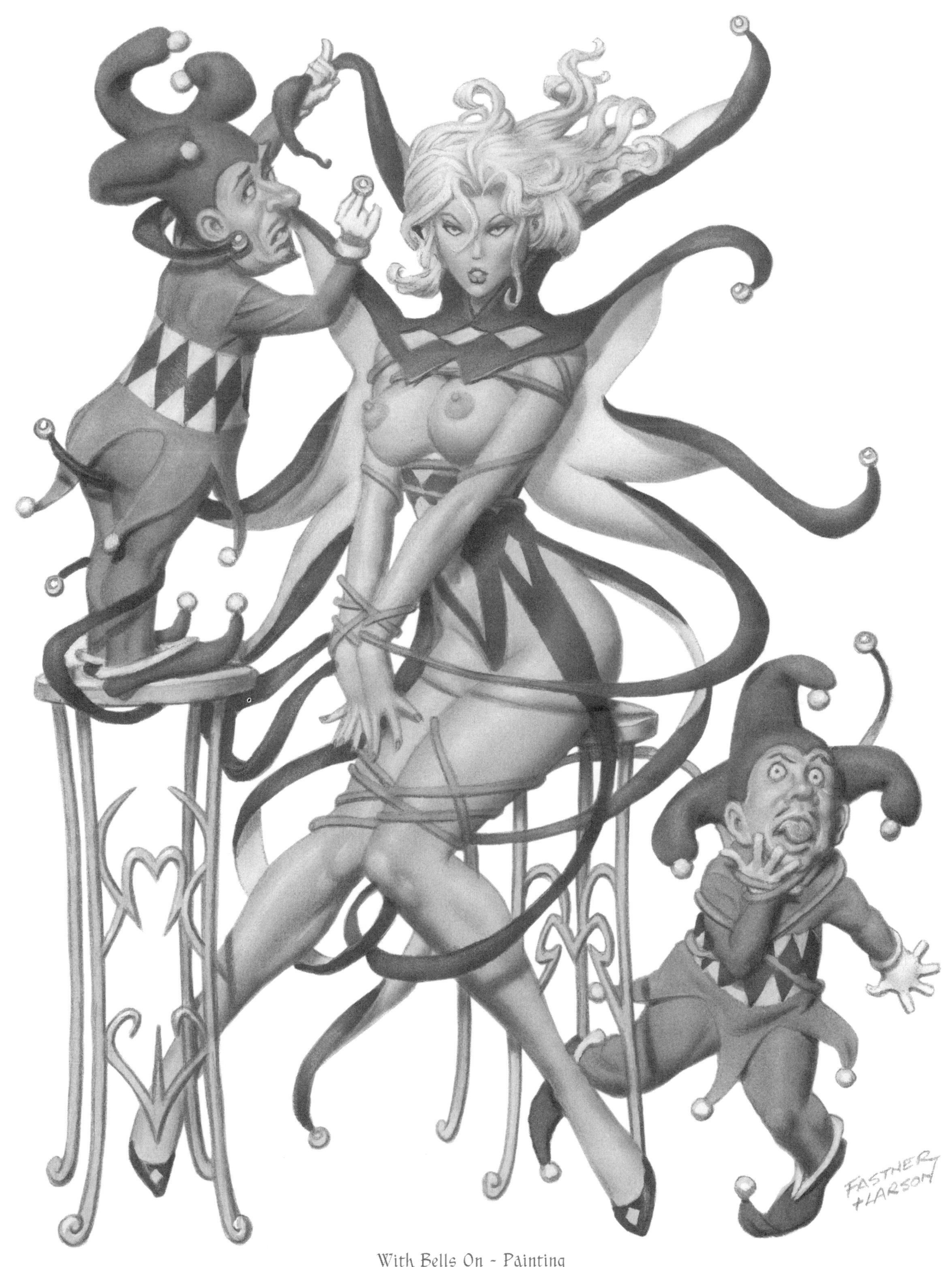

With Bells On - Painting

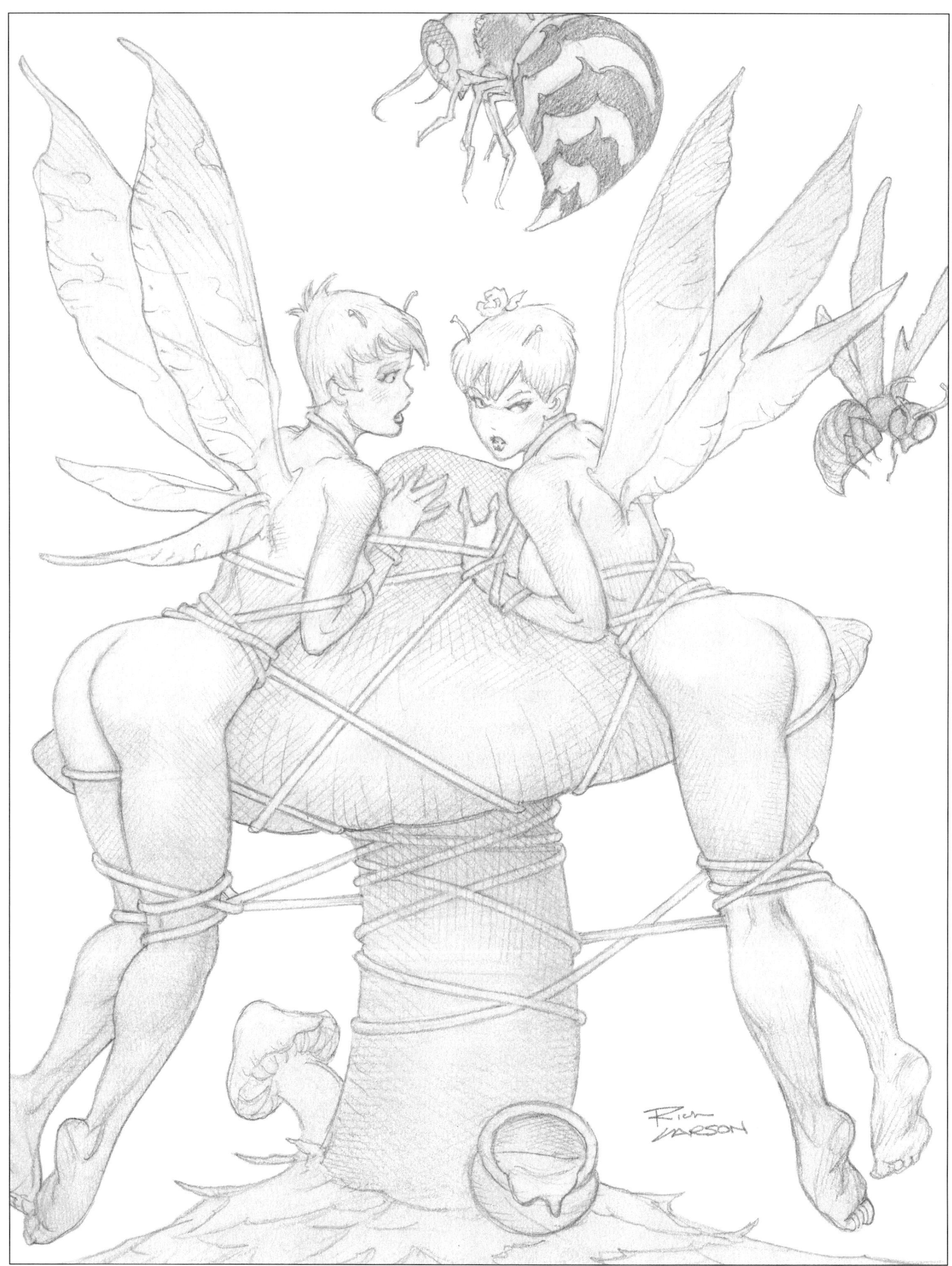

The Honey Thieves

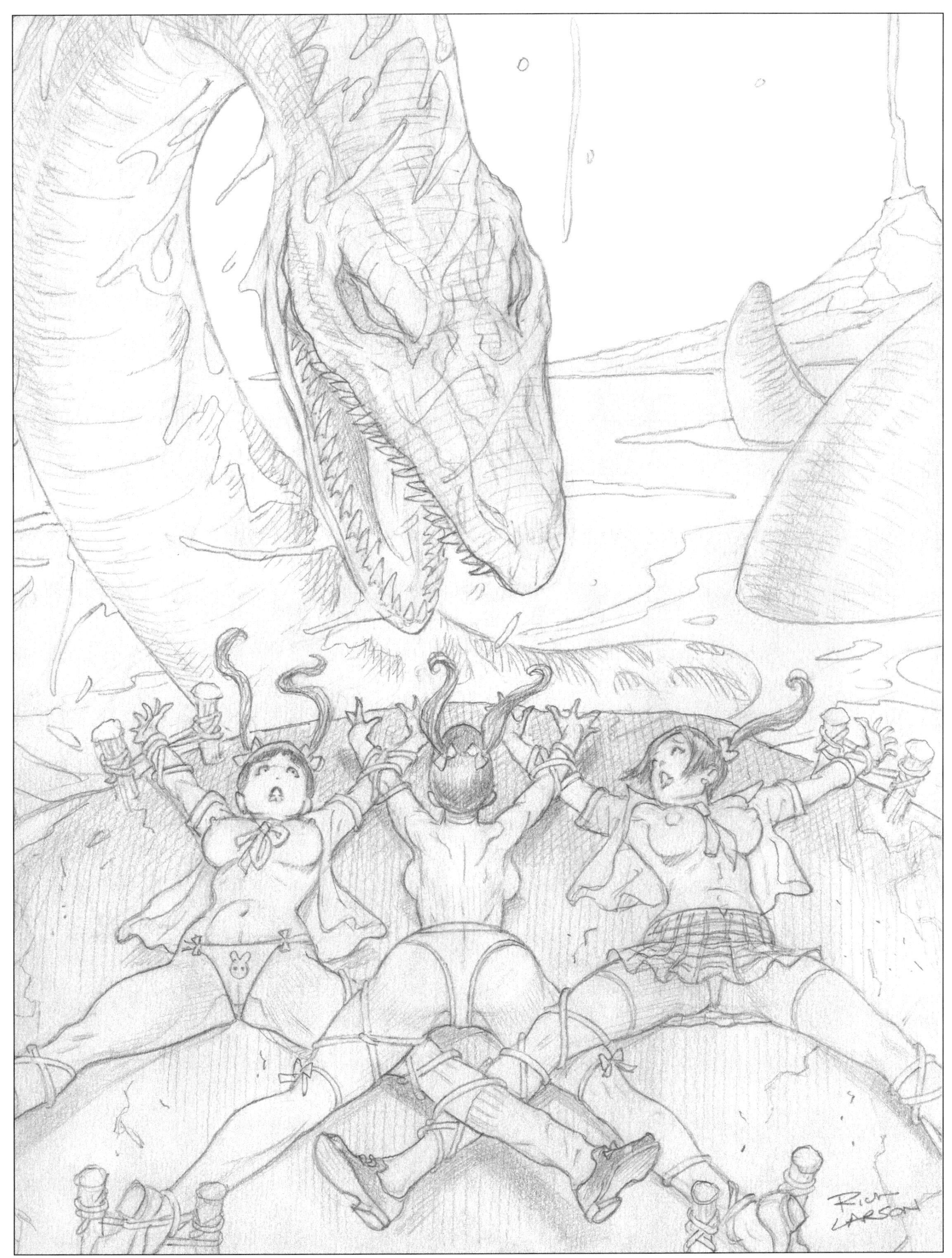

Schoolgirls of the Mesozoic

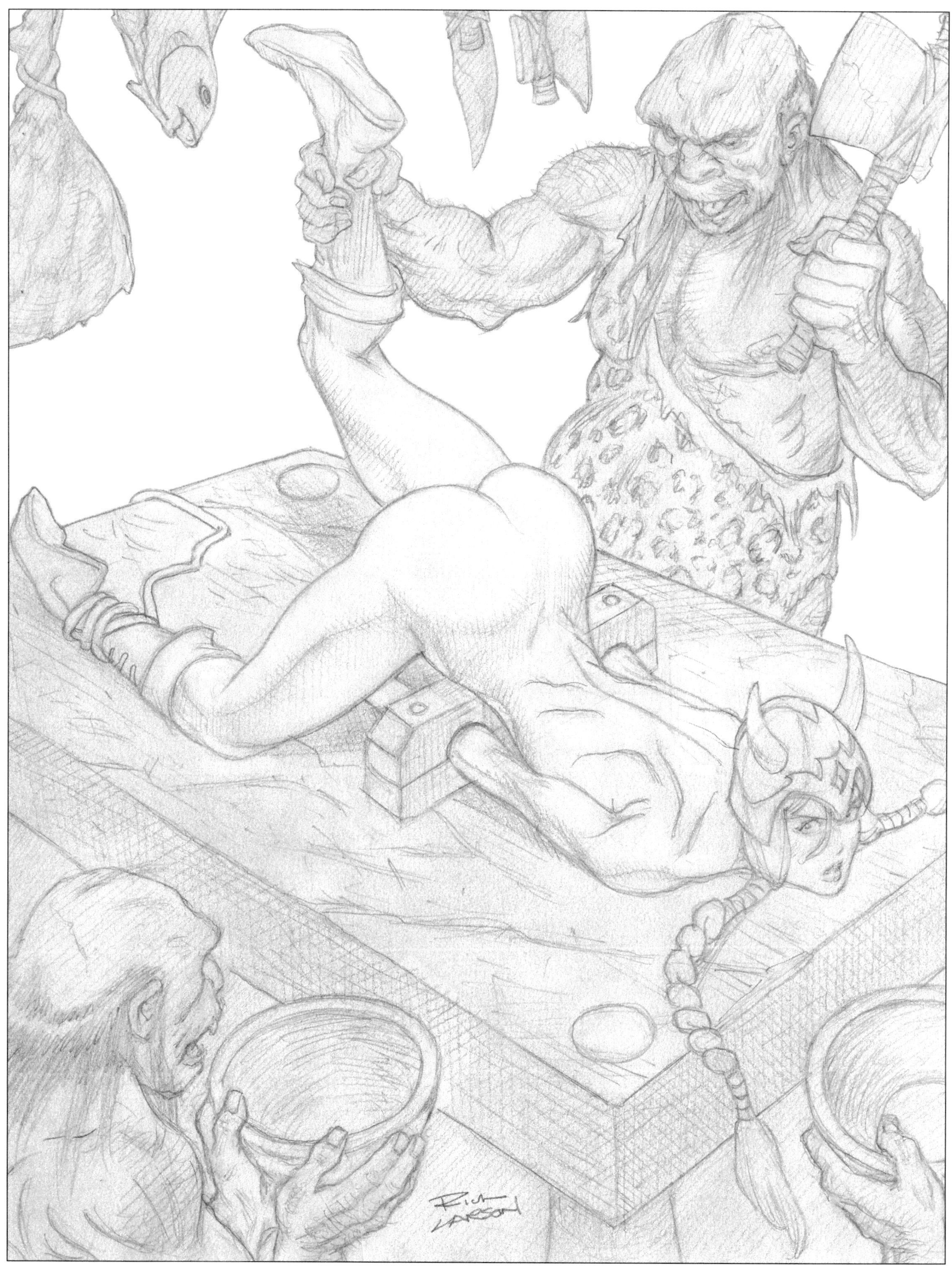

Horns of Plenty

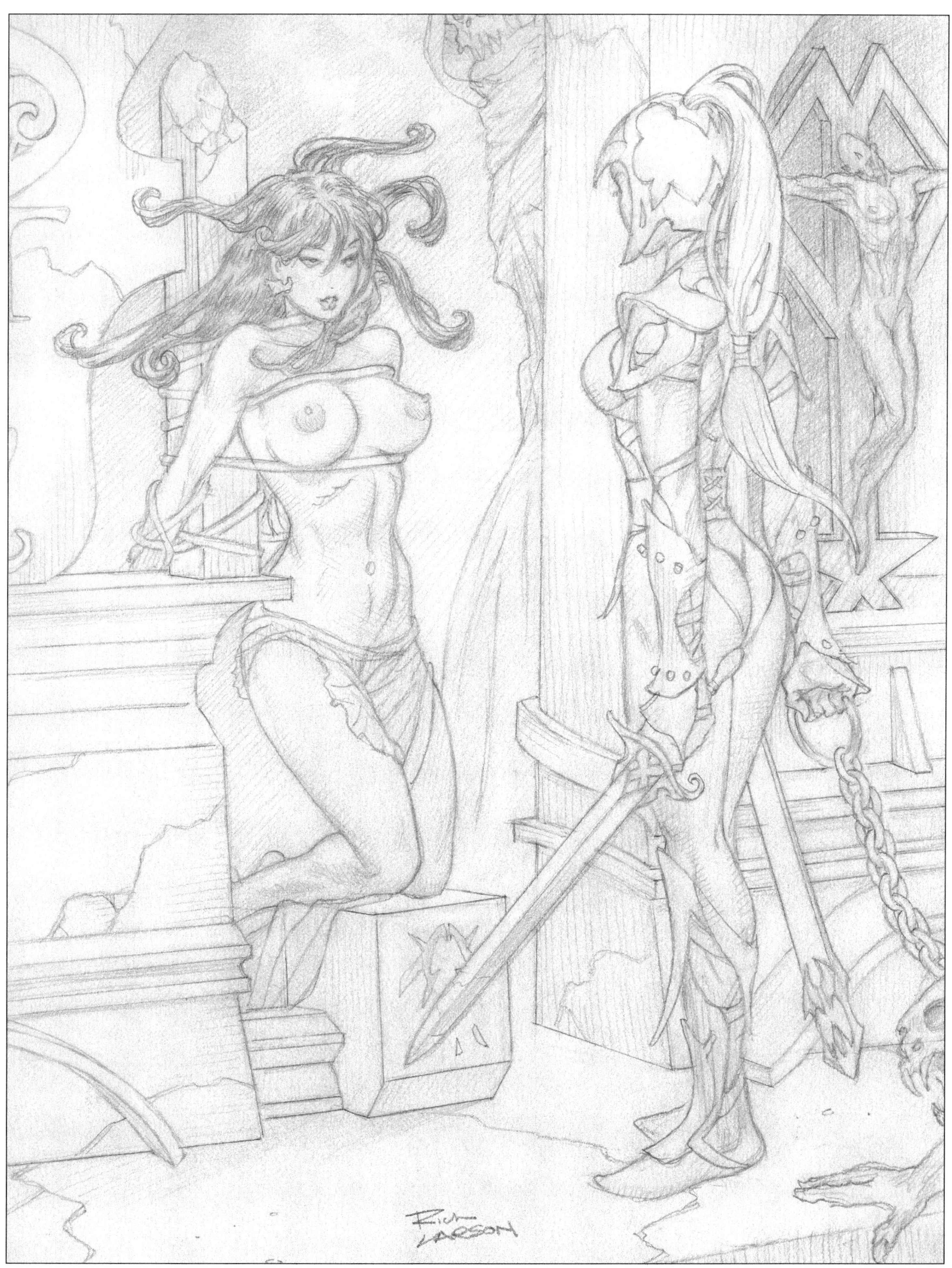

Prisoner Exchange

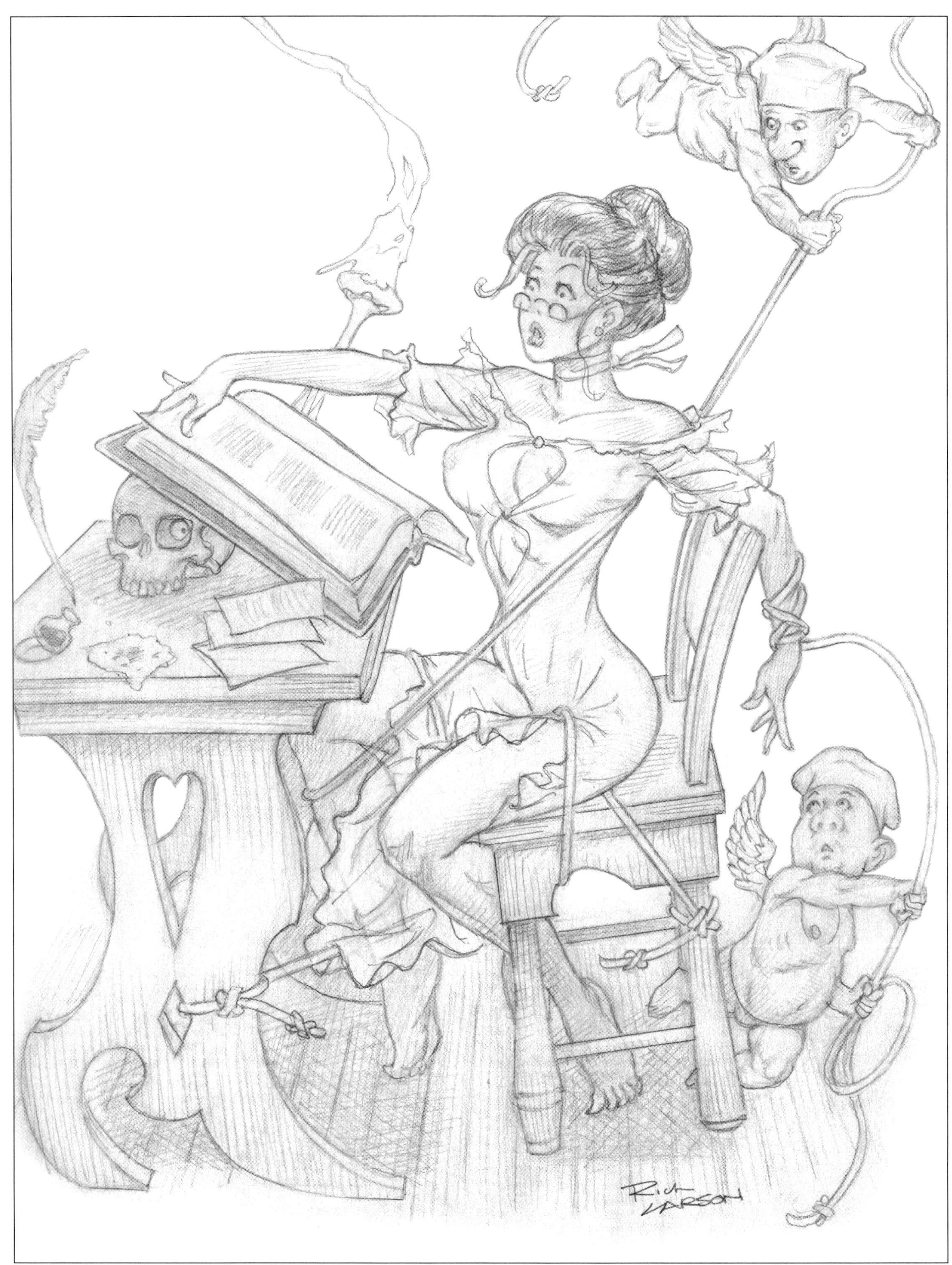

Devil's Cook Book

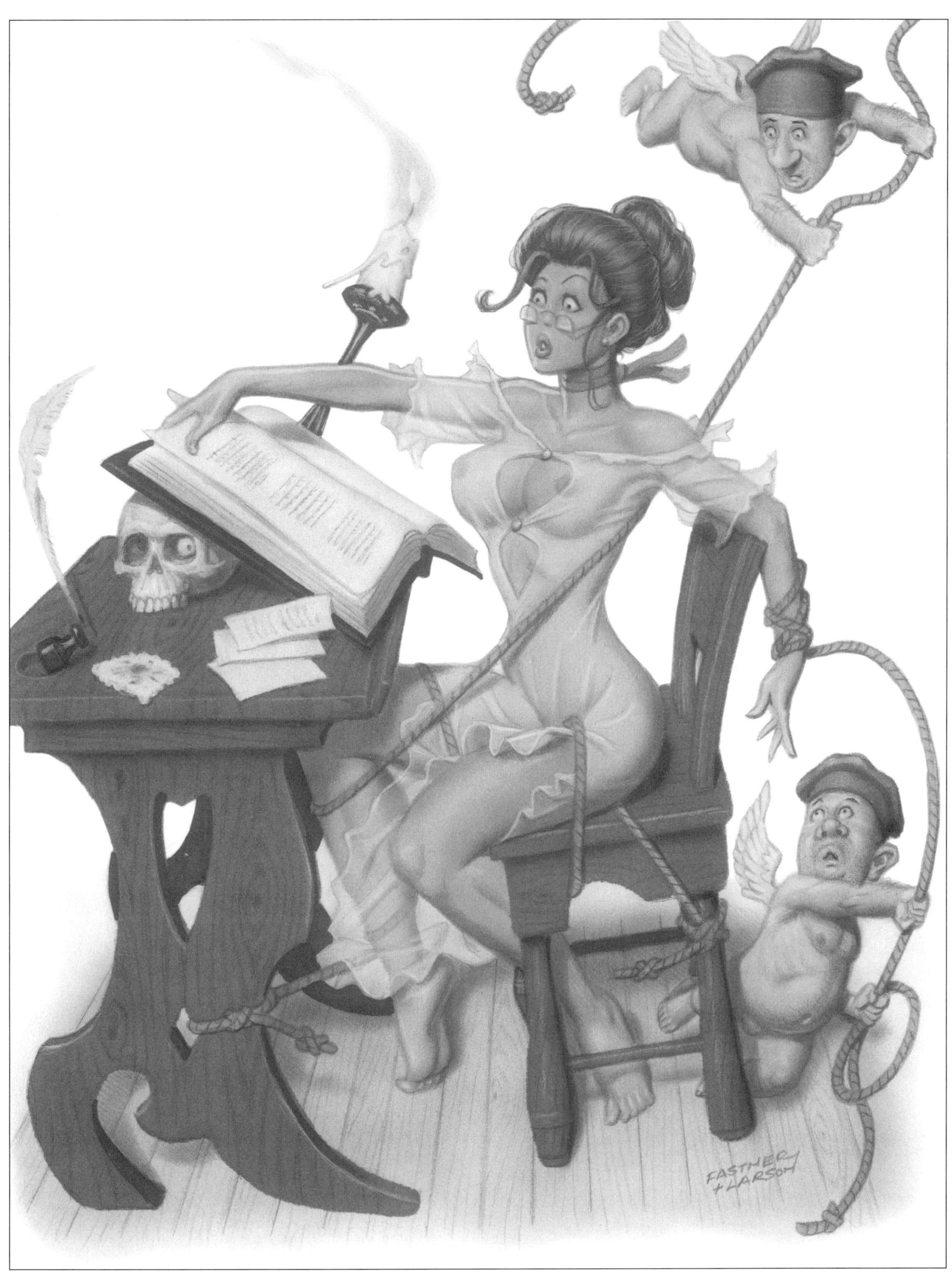

Devil's Cook Book - Painting

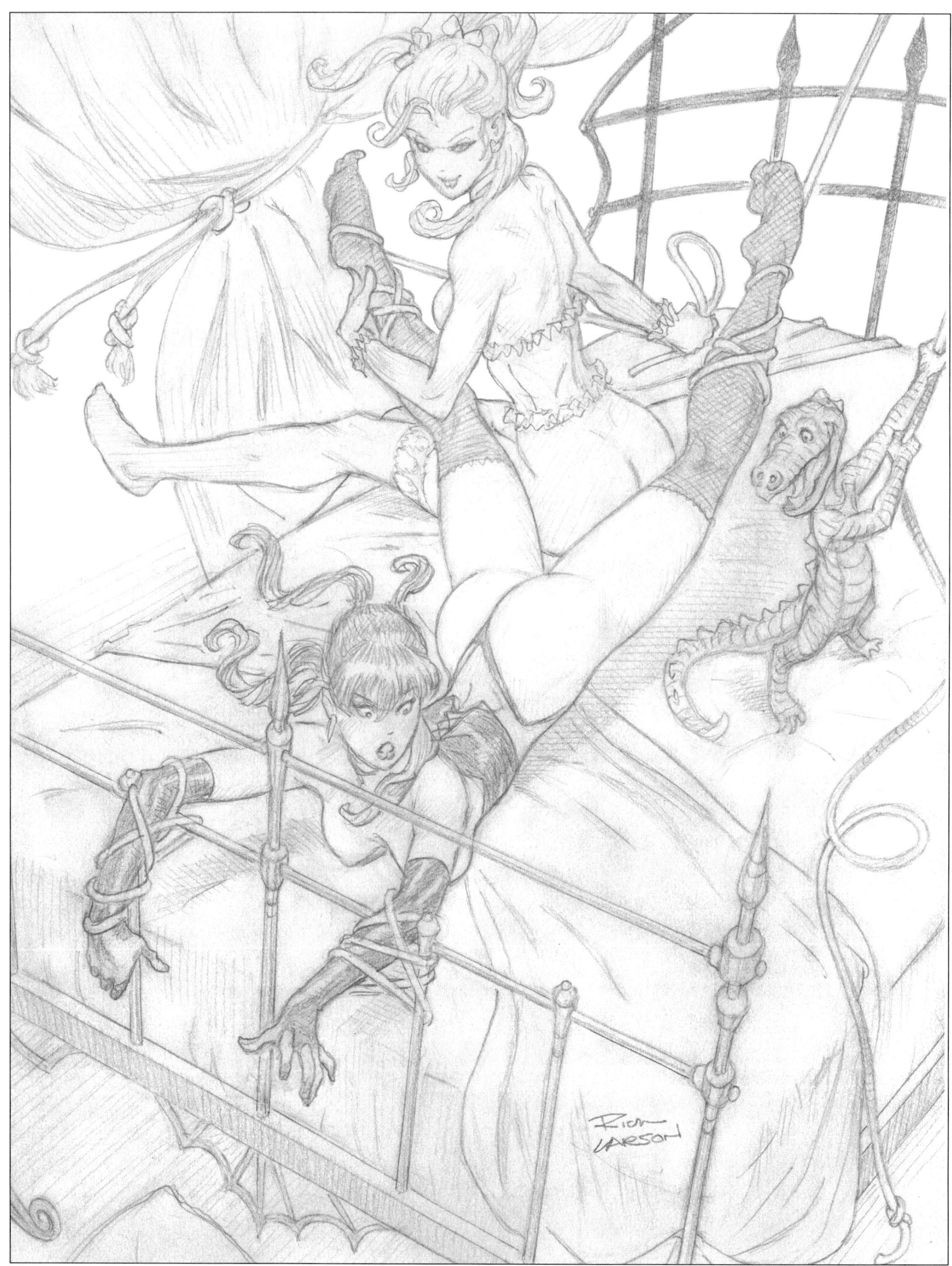

Night Games

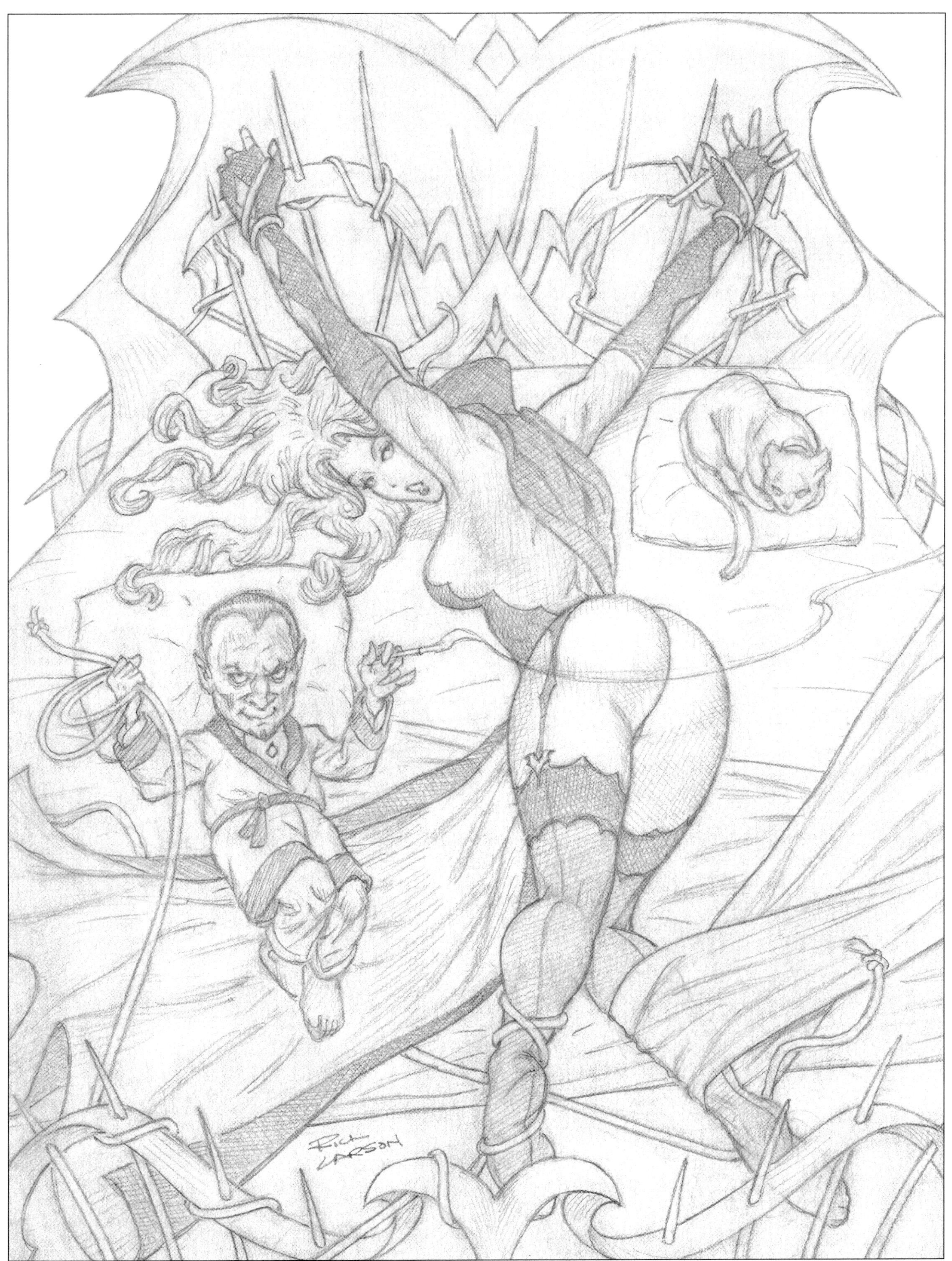

The Fun Couple

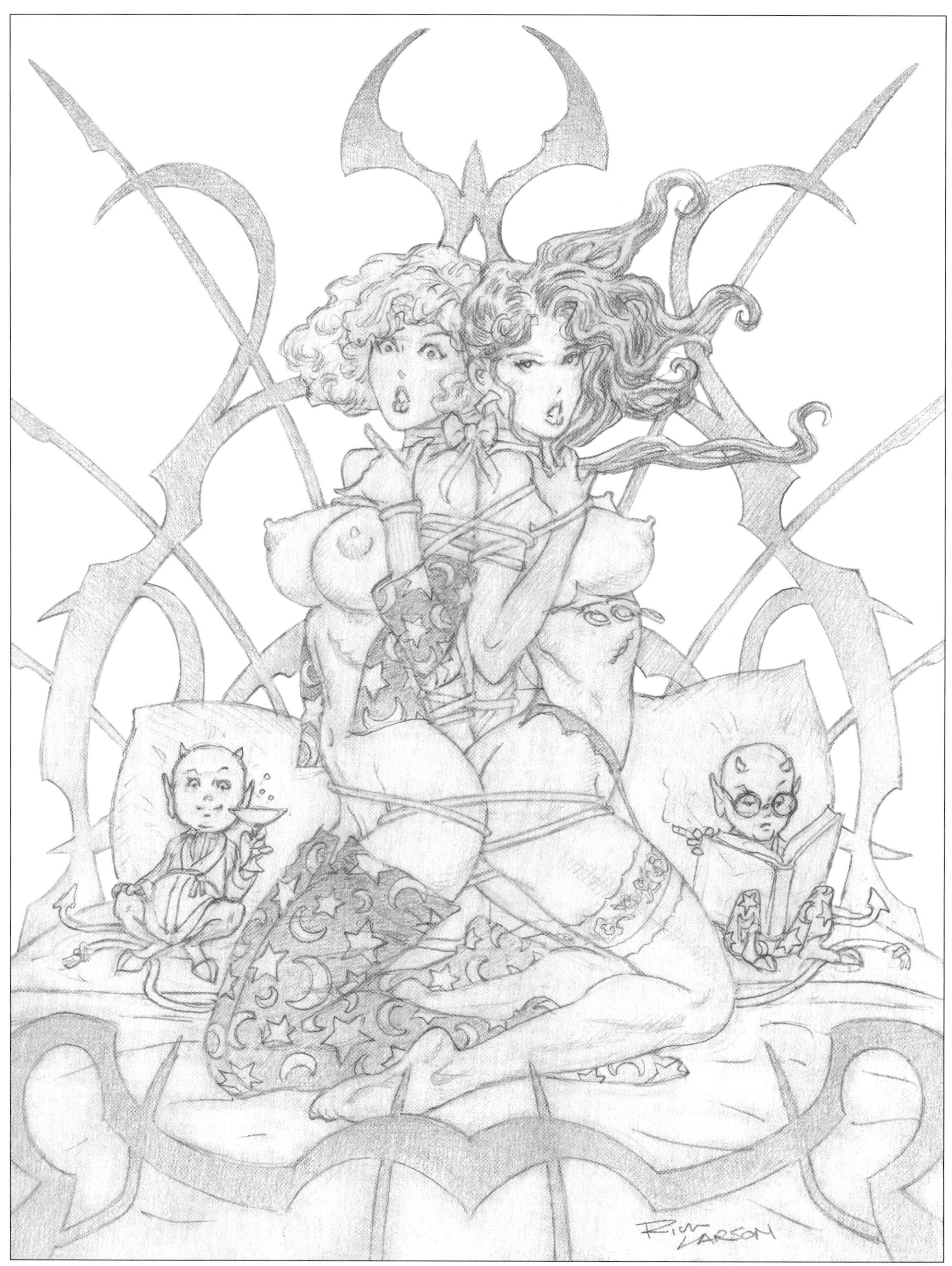

Strange Bedfellows

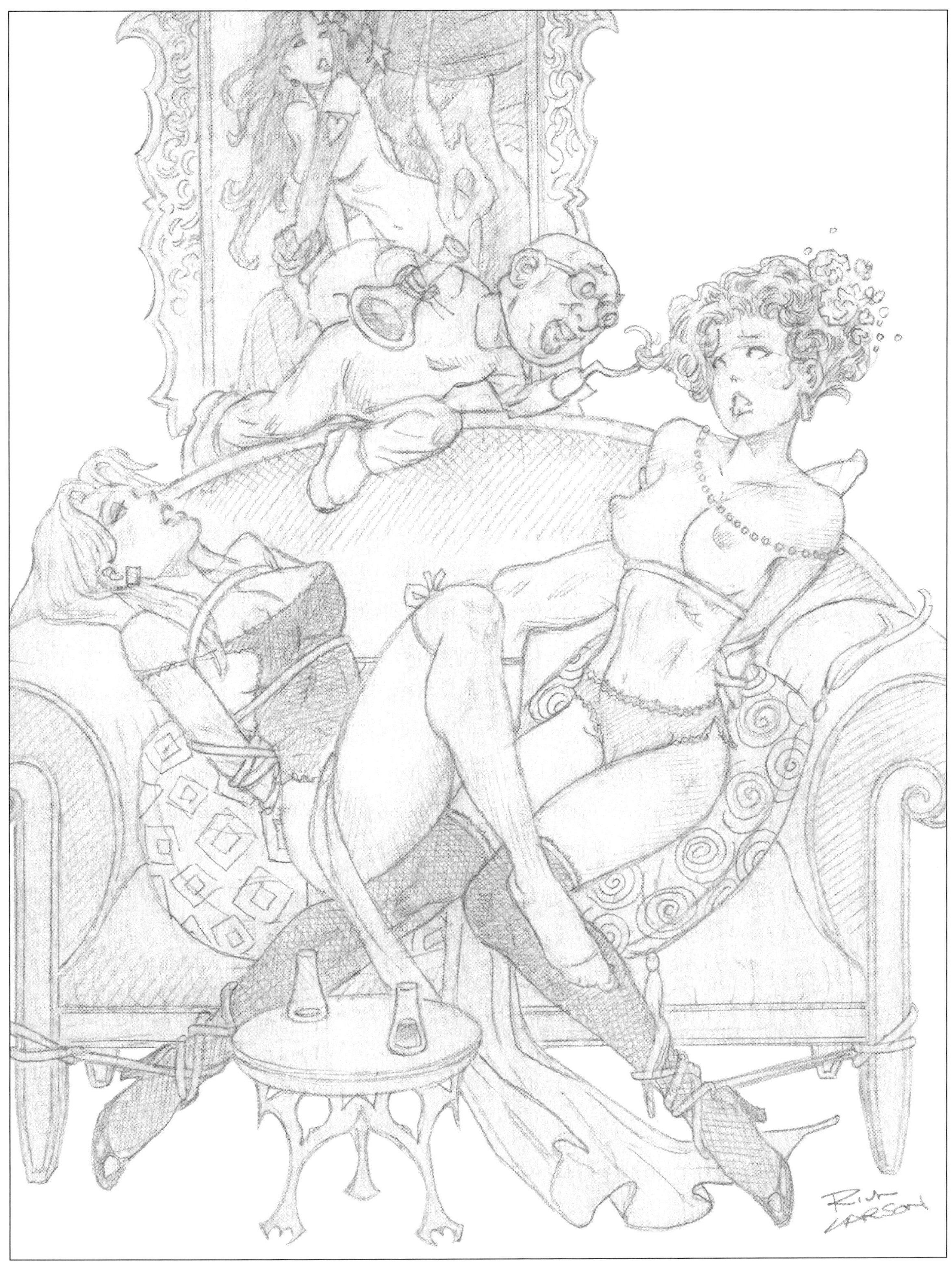

Night Cap

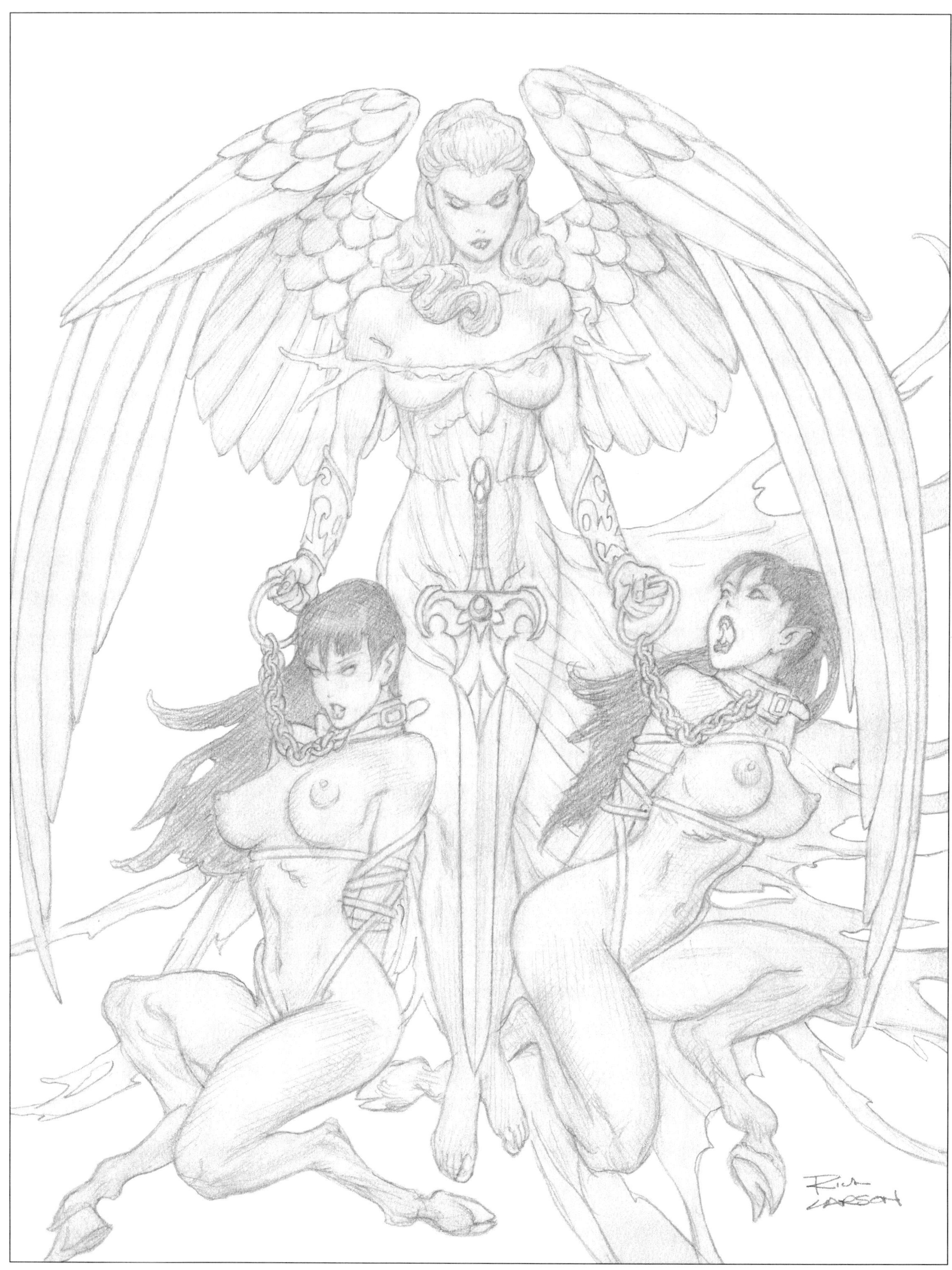

South of Heaven

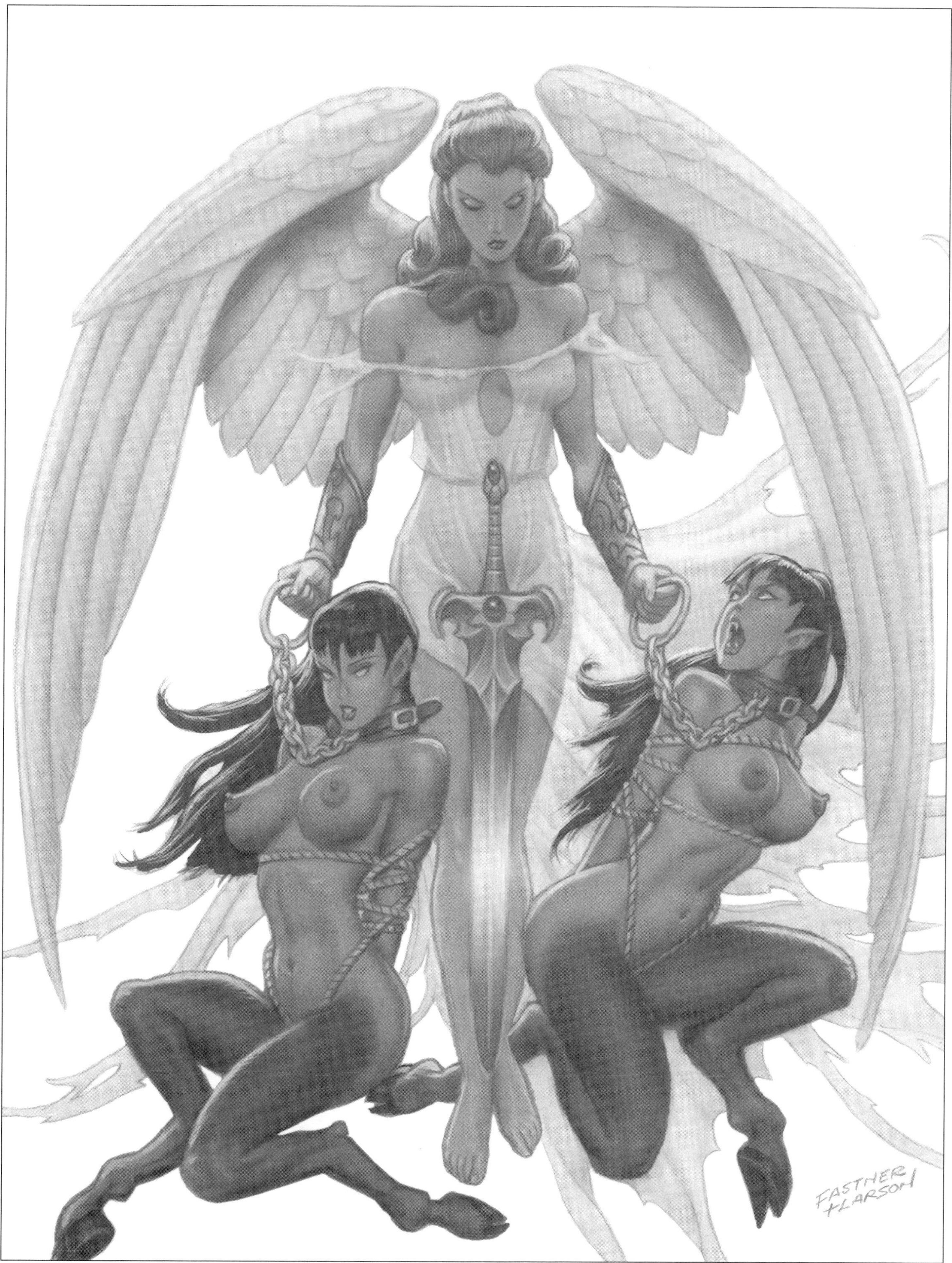

South of Heaven - Painting

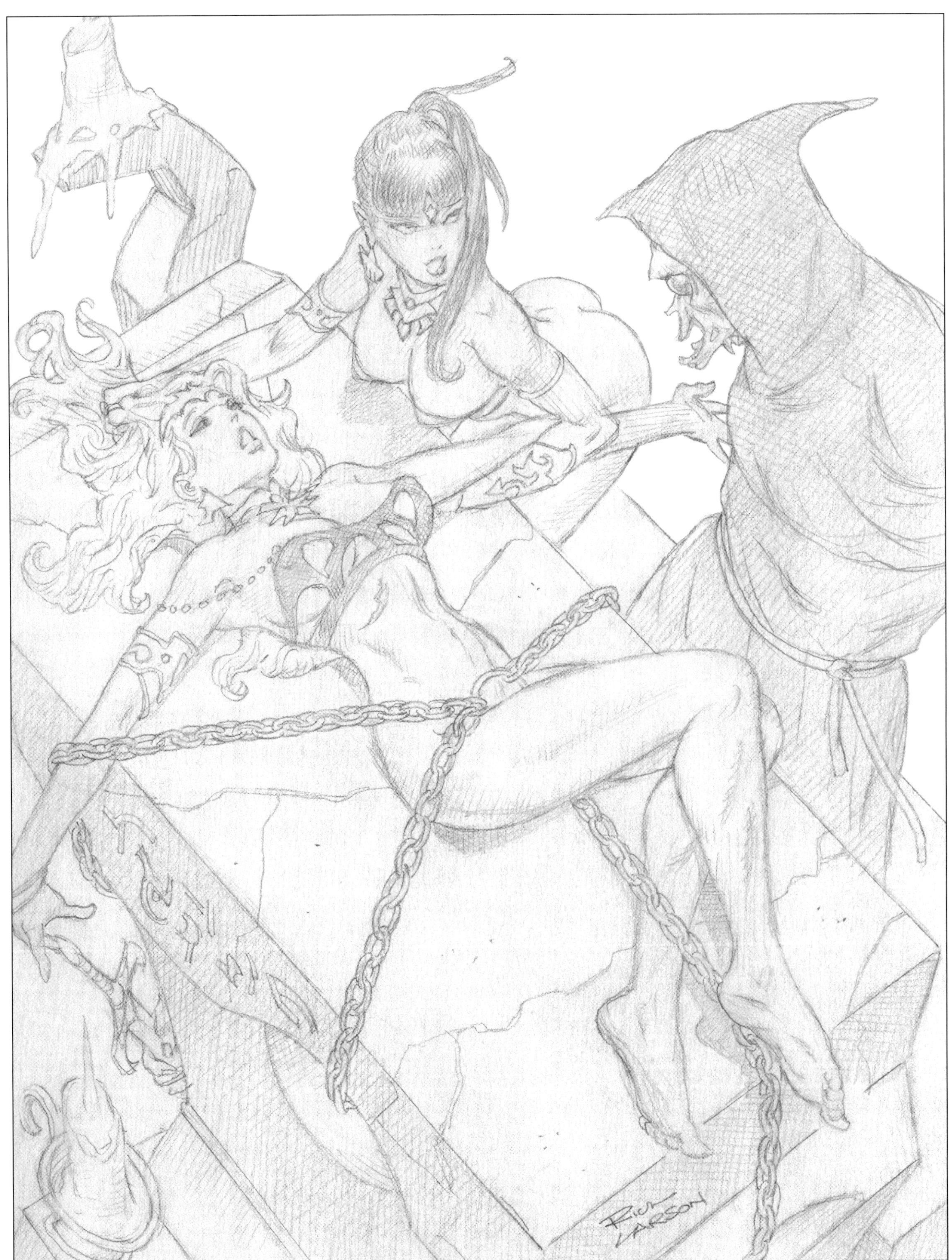

Fighting Chance

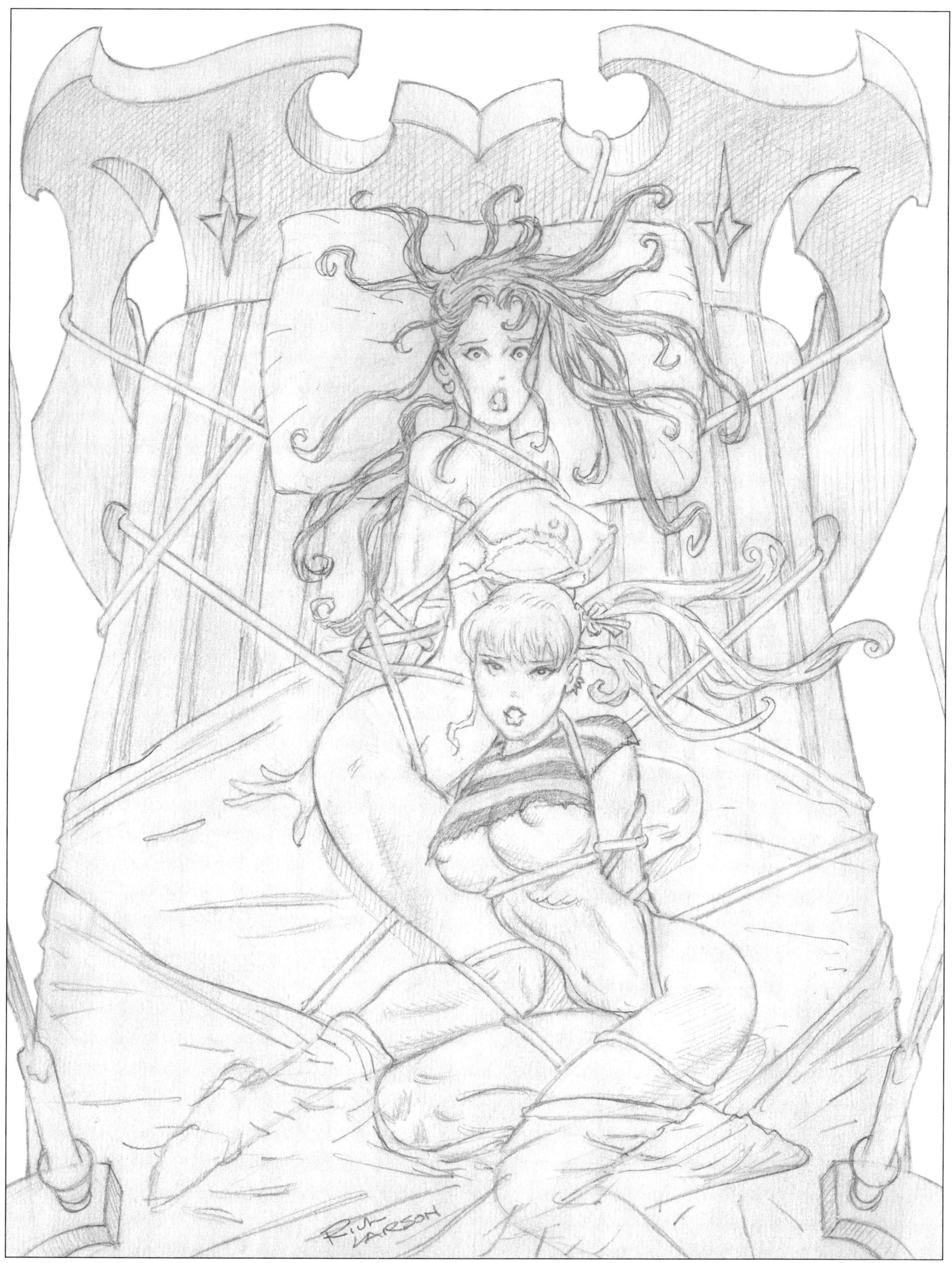

Light Sleepers

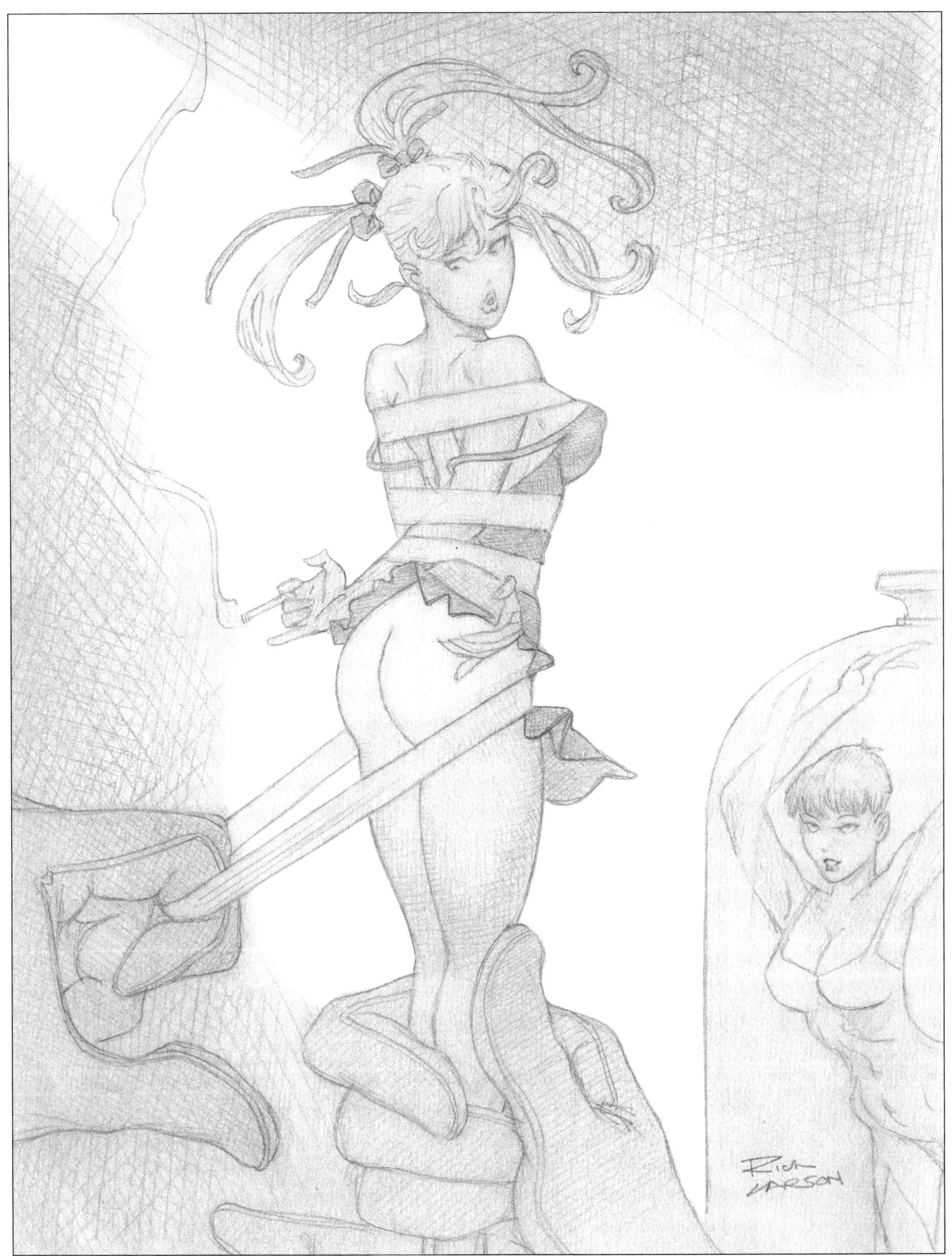

Oh Snap!